# ASIAN AMERICAN APOSTATE

"With irreverent humor and biting criticism, Scott takes us deep into the world of evangelical academics. His sharp writing style plies us with laughter as he takes direct aim at the entrenched prejudices of these closed spaces. Thank <insert deity of preference> I've crossed paths with this man and his writing!"

Keiko Agena, actress from *Gilmore Girls* and *Prodigal Son*

"I'd always seen Scott Okamoto around at community events, and wondered how an ex-evangelical man ended up in our radical lefty Asian American poetry and music spaces. In this easy-to-follow narrative, Scott outlines this journey, navigating his faith under the oppressive of weight of White supremacy and his discovery of Asian American identity to help him find himself again. As a Muslim American woman, I could relate to how a select few extremists in faith can manipulate people away from the critical thinking that all faith deserves. Through his writing, I gained insight about how over two decades Trumpism's specific brand of evangelicalism was incubated through prosperity gospel and prayer as a tool of White supremacy—insight gained only from teaching it at an evangelical university. Despite the racist hurdles at the university, Scott comes off as a passionate instructor who sees the best potential in every one of his students and only wants to develop them into critical thinkers and citizens of the world. Ultimately, this is a story of how art, and the journey to it, will save us all."

Tanzila Ahmed, political strategist, storyteller, and artist

"R. Scott Okamoto lost his evangelical faith, but he found his voice. Incisive, wry, and compassionate, *Asian American Apostate* speaks to the unspoken racial and social tensions that exist under the surface on White evangelical Christian campuses—not just for students, but for faculty and staff as well. A must read."

Blake Chastain, host of *Exvangelical*

"A deeply resonant chronicle of cultural shifts and personal awakenings, of losing faith and finding your place in the world—brave, brilliant, breathtaking."

Sarah Kuhn, author of the *Heroine Complex* series

"Scott Okamoto's harrowing and darkly funny account of the Christian evangelical sausage machine is an indictment of turning faith into political power rather than spiritual transformation. Okamoto's voice is necessary for times like these."

Naomi Hirahara, former editor with *The Rafu Shimpo* newspaper and Mary Higgins Clark Award-winning mystery author of *Clark and Division*

"Scott Okamoto's book is a triumph for those of us who fought for an education at a religious university. In its affirmation of our experiences of racism, homophobia, and misogyny at these religious universities, Okamoto weaves a narrative that is not only important for personal healing, but great institutional change."

Josephine Jael Jimenez, host of *Speaking in Church*

"R. Scott Okamoto's *Asian American Apostate*, in many ways, is a successor to great Japanese American authors like John Okada and David Mura. Okamoto's memoir is funny, punchy, and touches on a topic that Asian America typically does not cover—our relationship to evangelical Christianity. However, Okamoto's book is more than just a memoir about race, religion, and higher education, it is a story of ultimately staying true to one's convictions."

Naomi Ko, filmmaker, writer, and actor

"Scott gifts us not only with his story, but also with the experience of an Asian American man in the US. With perspicuous vulnerability, and considerate humor, he shares with us an account we all need to uncomfortably sit with. *Asian American Apostate* is a needed mirror pointed at very harmful realities lived by racialized people all over classrooms and pews."

Jo Luehmann, host of *The Living Room* and author of *Predatory God* (2024)

"Scott Okamoto's *Asian American Apostate* is a stunning contribution to the topic of deconstruction and leaving high-demand religion that for too long has been almost exclusively occupied by White voices. As an Asian American I am used to reading about Asian American experiences in one place and deconstruction narratives in another. Okamoto's work is groundbreaking for the way it injects the raw, unfiltered voice of a Japanese American ex-evangelical who gave all he had to the faith only to realize that its power brokers and rank and file citizens would never consider him enough. Okamoto tells his story with candor, humor, and honesty. It is the kind of book that makes you tear up in one instance, cringe in the next, and nod your head vigorously all on the same page. For Asian American readers and other people of color this will be like a balm on a wound that has been opened both by the abuses of religion and the travesties of racism. For White readers it will be an eye opening window into the multidimensional ways that people of Asian descent are treated as both pets, model minorities who are expected to show docility and submissiveness, and threats, perpetual outsiders who must be watched with suspicion."

Bradley Onishi, host of *Straight White American Jesus* and author of *Preparing for War: The Extremist History of White Christian Nationalism—and What Comes Next*

"As an exvangelical, I am deeply appreciative of *Asian American Apostate*'s take-no-prisoners approach to exposing the toxic nature of American evangelicalism. The American public needs these exposes, but Scott Okamoto's book also offers more. The wit, intimacy, and candor of Okamoto's prose make you feel like you're reading delicious disclosures from an old friend, and his journey of self-discovery provides readers with much needed inspiration, hope, and empowerment."

Chrissy Stroop, Senior Correspondent of *Religion Dispatches* and co-editor of *Empty the Pews: Stories of Leaving the Church*

"Scott's vulnerable and laugh-out-loud stories give us an insider's peek at the ironies and absurdities of American evangelical culture. *Asian American Apostate* is a must-read for anyone who cares about the important intersection of race and faith, and those who yearn to understand how our extreme culture wars have come to pass."

Jenny Yang, comedian and actor in *The Brothers Sun*

# ASIAN AMERICAN APOSTATE

Losing Religion and Finding Myself
at an Evangelical University

## R. SCOTT OKAMOTO

lakedrivebooks.com

Lake Drive Books
6757 Cascade Road SE, 162
Grand Rapids, MI 49546

info@lakedrivebooks.com
lakedrivebooks.com
@lakedrivebooks

*Publishing books that help you heal, grow, and discover.*

Paperback ISBN: 978-1-957687-13-1
eBook ISBN: 978-1-957687-14-8

Library of Congress Control Number: 2022948609

This book is memoir. It reflects the author's present recollections and information gathering of experiences over time. Most of the names of individuals or institutions and their characteristics have been changed, some events have been compressed, and some dialogue has been recreated.

*To Geri. This, like so many things, is only possible because of you.*

# Contents

# Foreword

As an agnostic who grew up in a Buddhist household, and as someone who actively seeks out conversations about religion, there is something that I particularly notice when speaking with two or more Christians (current or former) at the same time. They end up mostly speaking with each other. They forget to engage with the others in the circle. Perhaps this is because there is an assumption that the rest of us don't have much to offer in a conversation on Christianity, or perhaps there is so much trauma embedded in their experience, they seek to commiserate with others who have personal understanding from their own journey with the religion.

And yet, I believe it is near impossible for anyone growing up in the United States to escape a relationship with or orientation to Christianity, even if it is happening from a distance. To some of the points of *Asian American Apostate*, Christianity itself is so deeply embedded in this country's foundation and institutions—and the assumption of what it means to be "American"—that it is an active part of our formation as people in conscious and unconscious ways. Even just having to say the word *God* every day in elementary school during the Pledge of Allegiance was a practice of unwanted indoctrination. My decision as a third grader to remain silent from that point forward on "under God" was as much an act of private rebellion as it was a way to maintain sanity under the thumb of what I considered to be "this country's religion."

Reading *Asian American Apostate* is like sitting with a friend who understands how necessary it is to open the conversation to a much broader public.

I had visited EVU several times over the years along with other friends whom Scott invited to speak in class or perform at an event for EVU. I'll never forget my first performance for that campus.

I read a poem about people relating to each other (and me) through curiosity, desire, and queerness. While I was at the mic, someone who appeared to be a frazzled administrator type was running around near the entrance to the hall, behind the last row of the audience. He kept looking up at me and down at his phone, like he was desperately trying to get in touch with someone about what was happening onstage.

Before that evening, I'd known Scott was a secret advisor for the underground LGBTQIA club off campus, and of course I knew I was pushing the envelope—but I didn't know the extent to which anything queer was so completely off the table for public discourse at EVU. Needless to say, that was also my last time performing there.

While I take full responsibility for it going down that way, I also gratefully and wholeheartedly blame Scott for that night. From every previous class visit, I'd witnessed an excellent educator in Scott, who was challenging countless classes of students to think so far beyond the box, the Bible, and the system they signed up for. He was planting seeds in all of them—from the staunch believer to the genuinely open to the struggling future ex-evangelical. So how could I do anything less than step up to the plate Scott had already laid out for us to meet halfway with our actual, lived experiences, radical perspectives, and desires? (Yes, Scott, this was essentially your fault.)

And the students I met beyond the classroom—in the Asian Pacific American Student Organization and the secret LGBTQIA space—were not only thirsty for support and community, they were parched. Scott seemed as inspired by them as much as they were in gratitude for the way he held them up. As much as I felt for Scott enduring the weight of the EVU administration against him for so long, those students needed him, and their needs in turn kept him going.

*Asian American Apostate* will surely speak to the folks who have left EVU and left evangelicalism and religion altogether. It will serve as an extension of support to all those who were marginalized, fired, ostracized, and made to feel disposable at EVU and similar establishments across the country. This is also an invitation for society at large to grapple with the assertions on citizenry as dictated by systems and structures of power. This book is lovingly brazen on behalf of those escaping the institution as much as it is a book for the rest of us on the outside looking in. Thank you, R. Scott Okamoto, for being the professor we all desperately need and desire.

**traci kato-kiriyama,** author of *Navigating With(out) Instruments*

# Preface

Almost everything that happens to me, from the way I am perceived to the way I am treated, happens because I am a fourth-generation Japanese American man. Most of America sees me as a foreigner, and even though I don't speak Japanese, people are often surprised I don't speak with an accent. When people compliment my English speaking abilities, I tell them that four generations in an English-speaking country does wonders for one's English. It has become my nature to push back—gently at times, forcefully at others—at assumptions that deny my existence as a full-fledged American cisgender heterosexual man. Not that there's anything inherently special about such an identity. I learned to do this because I grew up in and worked inside of evangelical Christian culture. From a childhood in church to my job at a "flagship" evangelical university, I had to learn to choose myself and my communities, and I had to learn to flourish as a growing, caring human being.

This book is about exactly that. I went from being an embarrassing evangelical Christian to a theologically and politically moderate Christian to an agnostic person absolutely in awe of my heritage and my community.

It should go without saying that I'm not writing any of this book with an "Asian" accent, so don't go reading one. If anything, I might have a mild Southern California accent. I actually don't know if I do, but I wanted to plant an aural image into your mind. I'll circle back to this periodically, just to check in.

When I identified as an evangelical Christian, no one looked at me and assumed I was a Christian. Even after people learned I was a Christian, I was considered an Asian Christian, especially in evangelical settings. In "diverse" evangelical settings, my Asian American identity made me noticeable. "Diversity" in those settings always means "White" with a sensible amount of "not White," but "White" is still recognized as "normal" or "regular." Everything labeled as "diverse" in those settings is White-centered, encircled by "diversity."

My working at an evangelical university—which I'll call EVU—both "othered" me as a person and encouraged me to decide whether I wanted to just play the sidekick role of an "other," emasculated man, or go all in to my identity as a Japanese American. The Asians who are successful in White evangelical spaces lean in to the assumption that they are perpetual immigrants new to the cultural landscape who need to be welcomed by the benevolent White people. "New" people are just happy to be there. "New" people come into every room needing assistance or welcoming. "New" people don't encourage revolution or support students who push back at oppressive policies. "New" people take shit from White nationalist culture and ask for seconds. "New" people don't join subversive collectives or smoke weed with fringe poets.

I decided I didn't want to be a "new" person early on. I wanted agency to define who I was, and I wanted to be proud of who I was. My evangelical university's culture of White-centered bigotry gives all BIPOC people a choice: play to the assumptions of White people or fight like hell. So, instead of being seen as "new" at the university, I was labeled as "bad." Those are the only options in White evangelical spaces. You can be "new," and thus invisible, helpful, submissive, peacefully adding to the diversity, or "bad," and thus not fulfilling your role based on assumptions and biases in "superior" White minds.

Of course, I complicated matters by completely deconstructing my faith early on during my time there. To be clear, it wasn't the shitty White supremacy and all-around bigotry that made me "lose" my faith. It made deconstructing easier, to be sure, but that was not why I ditched my faith. I left because the Bible, to me, is a mess of contradictions that require Olympic-level mental gymnastics and PhD-level understandings of history and theology to form any viable guidance to a life today. All Christians, if they even study the Bible, have to pick and choose the things to follow and the things to ignore, or "contextualize." From the rabid Ku Klux Klan member to the thoughtful liberation theologian, a good chunk of "laws" and "sins" must be both followed and ignored.

The title of this book makes use of the word *apostate*. An "apostate" is a person who has renounced a belief or principle. I'm told it's a pejorative term in Catholic communities, but it seems a perfect word to describe all of us who fall under the "exvangelical" or "deconstruction" labels popular today. It's me. I'm an "apostate." Nice to meet you.

But this is not just a book about faith deconstruction. I'm here to tell a story of how I survived teaching at EVU, deconstructed all my faith, and formed a new identity as a person in community with people and places I never would have imagined as an evangelical. On the way to becoming this person, I discovered that the world assumes evangelical Christians are good people, and that this is just not true. While there are many good people in those churches and at schools like what I'm calling EVU, the evangelical faith is easily one of the biggest threats to democracy and a world that includes all races, religions, and identities. Evangelical culture is a White nationalist institution, and my story shines a light on this inconvenient fact.

One thing I learned way back in my undergrad years at UC San Diego in the late eighties and early nineties is that the path forward for my Asian American people groups must follow what is now known as the Black Lives Matter movement. If Black lives don't matter in

America, our lives don't matter. So, while much of this book details my journey of discovering and inhabiting my identity as a Japanese American, this journey is directly tied to the work already done and the work still to be done for Black lives. And Brown lives, and women, and LGBTQIA lives.

## THE SETTING

The school I'll refer to as Evangelical University, or EVU, claims to be a top-notch university, citing its place on the *US News and World Report's* yearly list of such schools. When I started writing this book, EVU occupied the illustrious number 170 spot, tied with another evangelical university that forbids dancing, divorce, and, basically, happiness. Ignoring the fact that most people couldn't even name 170 schools, in what world is being number 170 considered "top-notch"?

I went to the University of California San Diego when it was an up-and-coming school. Recently, my alma mater came in at number 37 in a year EVU slayed the rankings at number 170. UC San Diego has hundreds of preeminent scholars; American Book Award-, Pulitzer Prize-, and Nobel Prize-winning faculty; state-of-the-art research facilities in all the sciences; and a full-range of course offerings in essentially every subject area. In my English classes, I had guest lectures from Toni Morrison, Philip Kan Gotanda, and David Mura. I attended school-sponsored lectures given by astronauts, politicians, and scientists. As a freshman, I was encouraged by my party-animal dormmates to go hear Jonas Salk speak. The culture of learning and academics was palpable.

EVU, which is somehow an accredited school, has . . . none of those things. They do have mandatory chapel services three times a week. In these services, they hear all manner of Christian speakers tell them being gay is a sickness to be cured, sex outside of marriage is a sin, and racism doesn't exist or doesn't matter. Some professors have contributed to *Christianity Today* and the school's glossy magazine, *EVU Life*. Sciences are taught, but evolution is decried as a ruse of Satan. English is one of the strongest academic departments, but there are extremely limited course offerings outside of the White canon. Most semesters there are no courses covering BIPOC or women writers, and even when there are, they are often canceled due to lack of interest. There are film professors who don't allow students to watch R-rated movies because there might be nudity or sex in them. On its best days, EVU, to me, is equal parts third-rate university and fundamentalist Sunday school.

And yet, a bachelor's degree is somehow awarded at both UC San Diego and EVU. I'll spend the rest of my life pondering that.

The reason I'm telling you my story about my time at EVU, however entertaining the exposé portions are, is my hope that there are ways forward in this world from the bigotry and fear of the conservative mind, which I once claimed, to an inclusive identity that stands and fights for social justice and human thriving. Evangelicals are an insidious problem, but I hope this chapter of my life illustrates that some conservatives can be reached, and life after faith can be mind-blowingly fulfilling. Even if that life begins deep inside a "flagship" evangelical "university."

Okay, maybe the scare quotes are petty.

Still no accent, right? Rrrright? The *r* was pronounced clearly, right?[1]

Okay. Let's go.

---

1. In all seriousness, no disrespect to people who speak English with foreign accents. It means they speak more than one language very well, which is more than most people can say!

# 1

# Red Flags

## University of California San Diego, 1990

A group calling themselves the Church of Christ (previously known as the Boston Church of Christ)[2] was a cult that had been kicked off several college campuses nationwide in the late 1980s and early 1990s because of the damage it did to students. Their members started out inviting students to Bible studies that emphasized "discipleship." This discipleship would turn ugly as they demanded more and more of the student. If he or she tried to end the discipleship, the poor student would be subjected to harassment at all hours, intimidation, and guilt trips. Once they had you, they used brainwashing to force you to cut all ties with friends, family, and environment, forcing the poor victim to give all money and possessions to the church and move to another part of the country to continue discipleship. The president of my wife's sorority at UC San Diego got mixed up with this group, and her parents famously had her abducted and taken to be deprogrammed

---

2. Not to be confused with the International Churches of Christ.

1

by a psychiatrist. She returned a few months later, humbled and weak, telling people she could not eat at certain times of day or return to any of the routines she was programmed with, or else she could fall back under the spell.

At one point, the cult turned its sights on us InterVarsity Christian Fellowship folks, whom they considered heretics. Since I was the worship leader, they took to plopping down at my table in the student center while I was eating lunch to engage in discussion about Christian topics. I was well-read in pseudo-apologetics, having immersed myself in C.S. Lewis and Josh McDowell, so they were easy enough to fend off, but they were persistent, finding me all over campus and demanding I talk to them. At one point two Church of Christ members jumped out from behind some bushes near my on-campus apartment and began asking questions about worship. I was tired. I was tired of them. I had happily kicked their asses, theologically speaking, for weeks. And here they were, still coming at me. I said the only thing that came to mind, and at the time I felt bad for it.

"Just fuck off!"

It worked. They stared at me, mouths agape with nothing to come back with. I justified my profanity by thinking "God" had used it for "good."

## The *Playboy* Business

I first stepped onto the EVU campus for a job interview in fall 1998. As I walked down what I would later learn to be the Mascot Walk at the center of the main campus, groups of White students, mostly women, said hi to me. As someone who had attended a big state school, UC San Diego, I was immediately suspicious of this behavior. I asked one of the weirdly friendly groups where the administration building was, and they enthusiastically pointed me in the right direction. After I thanked them, one of the women said, "Blessings on your day!" I mumbled something like, "Um . . . you too."

I was disoriented for sure. I hadn't been in such a uniformly White space since I was a kid in elementary school, and I was not used to random strangers making eye contact, much less excitedly saying hi or extending blessings. When I walked the campus of UC San Diego ten years earlier, no one said hi to me who didn't already know me. The way regular, nonsociopathic people behave.

I walked into the provost's office armed with one semester's experience teaching at a community college, a minor literary award for a novel I wrote in grad school, and a lifetime mastery of evangelical Christian lingo. The provost was a friendly older White guy who seemed to like me. Early in our conversation, he lowered his voice and leaned toward me. "You've no doubt heard about the *Playboy* business."

I sat stunned. Did this administrator at a Christian school just refer to *Playboy* the magazine? I had been prepping my brain to speak evangelicalese, and I thought I was ready for anything, but a reference to *Playboy*? It felt like a trap.

Perhaps taking my silent bewilderment as consternation, he got flustered and said it was all overblown. Something about the student not being enrolled any more. He hoped I wouldn't hold it against the school or have any misgivings about working there. I would later learn from students that a former student had been nude in a college pictorial. The fact that she had attended a Christian school was what had made it "news." The internet was still in its prepubescent stages, so news like this didn't travel far and wide like it would have today.

I finally found my voice and told him I wasn't bothered by whatever he was talking about, and I wasn't lying. He let out a deep breath. "Oh, that's good then," he said as he sat back and straightened his glasses. He told me some other would-be applicants were appalled by the story, but I told him I didn't think it reflected on the school at all.

He was smiling as he handed me some paperwork to take to the English department. I had the administration's blessing to be considered for an adjunct position by the chair of the department. As you'll come to find out, though, the words *EVU administration* and *blessing* would not be associated again for me for the next fifteen years.

The chair of the English department was another older White man. He too was friendly and seemed to be excited at my being a part of his department. He explained how the class I was teaching, Freshman Writing Seminar, was taught and handed me some thick binders with information about department policies. From this I took it to mean that I was in. Yay.

I walked back up the Mascot Walk as a new member of the Evangelical University faculty. As I took in the campus, I said hi to students passing by because, goddamnit, I was local now. Despite feeling the thrill of landing a job, a part of me actually didn't want to be teaching here. I had looked down on friends who went to Christian schools when I was younger. To me, it was a form of hiding from the real world. The *real* Christians, in my young mind, ventured out to *real* places that needed redeeming or something. There was also a small but growing doubt in my gut that had started in college. Christianity was losing its sheen for me, and had been for the past ten years. For years I enjoyed sliding down the slippery slope of deconstructing the conservative views of faith and life from my childhood while leaning toward more progressive forms of Christianity, but that faith was weakening.

I still believed in Jesus and salvation in 1998. Beyond that, everything was a little fuzzy. Unlike most Christians, I was not satisfied with C.S. Lewis's book *The Problem of Pain*, in which he attempts to explain why there is suffering in the world. The short answer: because of sin. Sure, God feels bad for it. Sure, it sucks. Bad things happen to good people, and if a Christian is honest, it's often God causing the bad things. Ask a fellow named Lot. Or Jesus. The fact that there are "reasons" for them to suffer greatly does not help if you are the one

4

suffering or dying completely unaware of the reasons. Did Jesus know he was dying so Donald Trump could invoke his name to become president over two thousand years later? I guess that's another book, but other questions remained. Why do we turn to the Bible for science when there basically was no science when it was written? Why doesn't Jesus say anything about LGBTQIA issues if it's such a big deal? If women aren't supposed to sit quietly in submission as Paul wrote, how the hell are we supposed to know which rules to follow in the Bible? And if music is so damn important to Christians, why does most of their music suck so much?

I basically committed to the idea that I would challenge the conservative students to consider these questions and help them grow their faith. I would quickly learn that students don't come to places like EVU to be challenged in the sense that their *views* are challenged. They come to be challenged to be more "on fire" or "in love with Jesus." And no, my idea of challenging and theirs was not a good mix. I have fifteen years of scars as evidence.

The excitement of being hired to teach at EVU countered any doubts and questions for the time being. It felt like a sign from God that I was on the right path. Hi, students of Evangelical University. I'm your new English instructor. May God have mercy on your souls. Pass the whiskey. And the weed. Please.

## THE MAGIC OF "FUCK"

I was given two sections of Freshman Writing Seminar (FWS) to teach in the spring of 1999. I was teaching at two other community colleges at the time, so I had a full slate of classes. Only the lowly adjunct is happy to teach five or six composition classes, with all the prep and grading involved.

At one of the community colleges, I developed what I thought was a novel way to teach parts of speech. American high school students rarely have a grasp of how sentences work, and teaching the basic building blocks was my way of introducing writing and grammar. But it proved excruciatingly difficult to teach students those damn building blocks. During an attempt to teach parts of speech, a student blurted out, "English is fucked." I joked that he had just used an adjective to describe the English language. The student seemed surprised that I wasn't chastising him for using "bad" language at first, and then said, "Oh, I get it." I don't know if he actually got it, but the exchange gave me an idea.

I wrote several sentences on the antiquated chalkboard, each with "fuck," "fucking," or "fucked," and each employed as a different part of speech. "I don't give a fuck," used it as a noun. "That's fucking crazy," used it as an adverb. I don't remember the exact sentence I used to show a verb, but I remember erasing it quickly, lest someone walk in and see something like, "Go fuck yourself," on the board.

The "fuck" lesson worked like magic. Students told me they had never understood modifiers before. I couldn't make "fuck" work for prepositions, but it worked pretty well for the rest. I told the students that no one outside of a lame composition class was ever going to ask them what a preposition was anyway.[3] The normal students in community college classrooms delighted in having a professor write *fuck* so many times on a board. Entertaining and effective. A teacher's wet dream. Fuck yeah. (Exclamation.)

Despite growing up being taught that "bad words" were, well, bad, I had decided in college that such language was just using words in different contexts. Words were just words. Some were appropriate for given situations. Others might not be.

At EVU, almost everyone subscribed to the "bad word" point of view and not the different-contexts one. And *fuck* is about the worst

---

3. Can any grammarians confirm that saying "Go the fuck to sleep" uses "fuck" as a preposition?

word in existence to evangelicals outside of *liberal*. And despite a lengthy discussion to explain my view that language is a tool and words are just words, the students at EVU in 1998 did not appreciate the pedagogy behind my parts-of-speech lesson. I was, in a word, fucked (adjective).

In what would become, on average, a twice-yearly occurrence, I was asked to come to the office of my chairperson to answer to student complaints. Several students in each of the two sections and a parent or two had called the school to report profanity in an EVU classroom. My chairperson chuckled as he asked to hear my explanation. I appreciated that he didn't just assume I had cussed a blue streak and wrote random profanity all over the board. That would come later. After I explained the lesson to him, he laughed and nodded. He thought it was a creative way to teach parts of speech, but he told me it couldn't be done at EVU. I apologized to my classes and that was that. Fucking lame (adverb). Unlike back at UCSD, the word *fuck* would not prove useful to improving my life.

I know now that I was naive to try and use that lesson at EVU, but my perspective was not just about using a "bad" word. It was a worldview that prioritized what is actually important over what might be assumed to be important. To me, words mattered, but only to the degree of their effectiveness. *Fuck* could be overused or used to compensate for a deficient vocabulary, but it could also be just the right word. Outside of evangelical spaces, of course. It will also factor heavily in the end of my story. We call that foreshadowing.

# THE CULT RETURNS

Most of my students were great. They may not have agreed with me on most issues, but they were willing to listen and learn, and they showed respect to me as a professor. I would not have made it for as long as I did without them. At any school there are challenging students, but

EVU attracts all types of Christians, including some with extremely racist, sexist, or anti-LGBTQIA views. It must be pointed out, and I will do so for each example, that while these individuals caused me a significant amount of stress, anger, rage, and pain, I was generally able to make peace with them. And if any of them are reading this, I am writing this book as a testament to both them and me for being able to overcome such vast differences in worldview.

It was rare to have any Black students at EVU, but when I did, I always checked in with them to make sure they were okay amid all this racism. Grace was a Black student who understood how shitty EVU culture was. When returning to her dorm with her White friends, the notoriously racist White campus safety officers would stop her and demand she show her ID. They never asked the White students for their IDs. This happened most days for the first few weeks of her freshman year. She complained about White students always asking her if she was there on a sports scholarship or because of affirmative action; and as a prof at that time I knew that you only needed a C average and lots of money to attend EVU, so that question was especially galling. I leaned on Grace for support whenever race issues came up, enjoying rare moments of not having to be the one to bring up racism in evangelical culture. We often talked after class, joking about the clueless White kids, some of whom admitted that we were the first Black and Asian people they had ever gotten to know. One kid even admitted he had never talked to a Black or Asian person before . . . in his whole life.

About halfway into the semester, I began the first part of my lessons on argumentation. I wrote a few suggested discussion topics on the board and asked if the students had any topics they had been thinking about. Coming up with topics was practice in developing thesis statements, which are assertions to be supported with an academic paper.

Someone brought up worship and worship styles, bringing up the point that there were Christians who didn't like the EVU style of worship with its loud guitars and drums. Grace chimed in, saying she couldn't understand how people could worship at the school's chapel. It should be noted that the worship music and worship team were almost universally beloved at EVU. They had adapted the new trends of having polished musicians audition to be on the worship team and had attractive, male leaders. Grace raised her hand and told us EVU worship went against God.

Grace's comment confused everyone and made my spider senses start tingling the same way they did when confronted by the Church of Christ nut jobs. She started quoting scripture about worship, but none of the verses said anything about guitars and drums. Someone asked what church she went to, and Grace seemed to be expecting the question. "I go to the one true church of Christ," she said confidently, if casually. It was like she was saying, "Oh, you know, I go to Calvary Chapel."[4] Except she didn't go to fucking (adjective) Calvary Chapel. She went to the fucking "one true church." Someone asked what kind of church it was. Grace laughed, condescendingly, and repeated, "It's the one true church." The students looked confused. I felt my heart pounding. My favorite student of the first few weeks was a member of the goddamn Church of Christ. My mind raced back to my college days feuding with that church, and I made plans to alert the school that the students were in danger of being lured into a cult. And then Grace added that we who worshipped in places like EVU chapel were going to hell. *Hell.* As if that weren't weird enough, she seemed happy when she said it.

I don't think most of the class ever got their minds around the fact that one of their classmates had just said they were going to hell, or if they did, it did not fully dawn on them that their egregious sin was not homosexuality, tattoos, or liberalism. They were being sentenced to hell for one of the very foundations of evangelical Christianity: contemporary worship.

---

4. Basically the McDonald's of evangelical churches with branches all over America.

In my mind, I was convinced that the best way to deal with these people was to come hard and come strong. I said to the class (and I know this because it was documented in a legal threat to the school), "Well, I guess I'll see you all in hell."

I spent a few minutes assuring the students that singing worship songs would not send them to hell, but I didn't directly address Grace. She sat looking stunned and saddened. I was stunned and saddened that I had to shoot her down like that. After class she stormed out of the room instead of chatting like she had every day before. She sat silently in class for the next couple of days.

Standing next to the door to his office, my department chair was waiting for me a few days after the incident. He invited me into his office for the second time in a year and a half, but this time he seemed genuinely worried.

He sat at his desk looking down at an official-looking trifold letter printed on official-looking stationary. He then handed me the letter and asked for my side of the story.

The letter was from the pastor of a local Church of Christ who was also the father of Grace. He detailed, word for word, some of what I had said in class before going on to say that unless amends were made, he would bring some kind of harassment lawsuit against the university. He did note that I was his daughter's favorite professor and that she was particularly grieved by the whole incident.

I told my side of the story, including my previous dealings with the church. My chairperson was clearly sympathetic but also keenly aware of the precarious position he was in. His instincts were to support me, but a lawsuit against the school could be serious trouble for everyone.

To make things better, I volunteered to take one for the team by submitting to the terms of the letter and apologizing to Grace and to the entire class. The next class session, I started out by apologizing for what I had said. I knew what was at stake, so even though I was not sorry at all for defending my students and their salvation status, I apologized to the class for my unprofessional conduct. I covered all the bases. Grace's father wrote another letter later in the week indicating he was satisfied with the outcome. No lawsuit. You're welcome, EVU.

The lack of response of the rest of the class was epic. As I apologized for being so insensitive and mean, they just stared blankly at me. Allowing for the fact that it was obviously unsettling to see their English professor apologizing so wholeheartedly, they said nothing. I asked if anyone had questions or comments. Nothing. I never figured out whether they were just not fazed by the whole incident, or if they just couldn't comprehend what had gone down.

Grace, herself, acted as if nothing had happened after that day. She talked during and after class about everything, including the rampant racism at the school. She defended many of my critiques of Christian culture and gave overwhelming support to my view that the campus climate was overtly hostile toward ethnic minorities. She even took another class with me the next year. And when Facebook went active on campus, she friended me. Go figure. A couple of years later, she amazed me, yet again, with her violently erratic worldview when she informed me that she was entering a city swimsuit competition and asked me to pray for her to win. Given our past conflict with contemporary worship as a contentious issue, I timidly asked her what her church might think about entering a swimsuit competition. She wasn't sure, but she was convinced God wanted her to do this. If I hadn't already arrived at a point where I stopped trying to understand this person, I'm pretty sure I did then. Perhaps for the best, I never saw her again after that day.

Outside of nearly getting the school sued, those first couple of years at EVU were surprisingly great experiences. Many of the full-time professors, including the chair, mentored me. By 2001, I was teaching the maximum number of units an adjunct could teach, three classes in the fall and two in the spring. I was able to stop teaching at one of the other community colleges, cutting my weekly drive time significantly. Things were looking good. The full-timers told me to consider getting my PhD so I could join full-time. Some even had their educations paid for by EVU, and they encouraged me to inquire about that.

Every administrator I asked about this said they knew nothing about such a program.

## Teaching Writing?

When people talk about good writing, I'd be willing to bet they cannot tell you exactly what they mean. They might mention a famous writer or the infamous White and Strunk text *The Elements of Style* as a reference. But what exactly good writing is? Hmm . . . If you went to college and took a composition class, there is a 74 percent chance that your professor or instructor had no idea what he or she was doing (*Scott's Educated Guess*, 2022). There is also a 63 percent chance that those same professors thought they knew what they were doing (*Pulled from Scott's Ass, 2022*). If you just noted that the previous sentences were not correctly annotated by APA, MLA, or Chicago style guides, you are probably part of the problem. Or you got an A in English Composition 101.

It was the pursuit of figuring out how to define, teach, and assess "good writing" that contributed greatly to my deconstruction from faith. For me, communicating clearly and artfully a person's ideas and points of view was the most important component to writing well. But if a person's point of view was that of an evangelical Christian, that person might never be a "good writer" in my class. Because an evangelical Christian likely has a deplorable and indefensible point of view, logically and ethically. It can be subjective, yes, but can a piece of writing be given an A if it is arguing for the validity of the Ku Klux Klan or that science is a ruse of Satan? Not in my class. Pretty sure you can do that in a lot of other classes at EVU, though.

This brings up the other part of the teaching equation: assessment. Teaching writing should correspond with assessing the writing. Stay with me here. An assignment that asks a student to write something should be accompanied by a class that equips the student to satisfy the outcomes and objectives of the assignment. And then, after a lengthy process of drafts, revisions, and editing, that writing must be measured against the parameters of the assignment. It should be clear to the student at every step of the process both what is being asked of the student and where the writing stands.

Okay. You now understand the basics of teaching writing according to me. Like all the Freshman Writing Seminar classes, assignments were based around the texts we chose for our classes. After going through the various kinds of college papers, the focus of the second half of my class was on argumentation. After one paper where they wrote an argument on an assigned topic, I then let the students choose from a broad list of topics. I also let them come up with their own topics that would need my approval. It was always fascinating when students disregarded my veto of their topics and went ahead with their papers, armed with assurance that Jesus was on their side.

I quickly discovered that an evangelical student has a harder time learning "good writing" than a camel trying to get through the eye of a needle. Even if we subscribe to one of the modern interpretations that the "eye of a needle" is a metaphor for the narrow gate of a walled city, and a camel laden with bags atop its hump must have its cargo painstakingly unloaded and reloaded to pass through, the metaphor still works. Evangelical students had to shed their evangelical biases, assumptions, and shitty worldviews to "write good." At least in my class they had to. I later learned that a lot of adjuncts teaching Freshman Writing Seminar were just having students write trite Christian messages and regurgitations of Christian writings. These were usually professors from the School of Business.

So even if a student figured out where nouns and verbs go in order to form a sentence, that student was still a camel with bags piled high trying to enter through a very small gate. Now, tell that student to write a thesis statement, the defining idea of every piece of college writing, and you might get statements like, "America's problems are all a result of taking prayer out of schools in the sixties," or, "In this paper I will prove that President Obama is, in fact, a Nazi." No matter how grammatical, how eloquent, how artful the words following thesis statements like that, I could not assess them as anything but deficient. Even when I considered myself a fellow Christian, there was no fucking (adverb) way pathetic ideas like those, and many others worse than they, could be considered "good writing." (Yes, "they" is the correct pronoun. Look it up if you must.)

To their credit, some diehard conservatives refused to heed my notes on their drafts and just turned in final papers with the same shitty arguments. Sometimes they would be accompanied with a note imploring me to prayerfully consider the godly truths in their papers. I did not need prayer to see the obvious. Those papers never received anything higher than a D. I still needed them to write good things on evaluations, so it was rare for me to give Fs. If I didn't need them to fill out the evaluations, I would have failed about a third of my students. No joke.

One of the students who tried the "prayer in schools" topic even confronted me in a moment of sheer self-owning delusion. She slammed her D-minus paper down and proclaimed that this same paper had received an A in her honors English class . . . in high school. Christian high school, obviously. Somehow, in her mind, she was going over my head by invoking the more godly assessment of her high school teacher. She was definitely going over my pay grade, but goddamn, kid. You just admitted that you didn't write this paper for my class. I told her the paper then deserved an F for plagiarism, but that she could keep the D-minus. When she realized what she had just admitted to, she was fine with the grade. I had pointed out early in her writing process that "bad

14

things," like slavery, wars, famines, diseases, and natural disasters, actually happened prior to the 1960s when prayer in schools became an issue. That this fact negated the whole argument couldn't sway her thinking, but a self-admission to plagiarism did. Self-preservation always trumps deeply held evangelical convictions. The 2016 election of Donald Trump proves that pretty well.

## There's Something Happening Here

After a few years of teaching Freshman Writing Seminar, my own faith was fading. These students were Christians just like I was. Except they were nothing like me. Nor were their parents, many of whom wrote to me to express their dismay in my teaching and grading. Again, most of the students enjoyed my class and the discussions we had to prepare for their papers. On student evaluations of my teaching, many wrote praise, saying I'd helped them become more thoughtful about their Christian faith.

But as the 2000 presidential election came and went, I started to see a dividing line between me and the students. Most students had little interest in politics, often claiming their faith came first and foremost and being Republican came second. Many conservative students willingly, if begrudgingly, pointed out that Jesus would likely be considered a "liberal" if he were alive at the time. But it was the intractable students who kept me awake at night. Nothing seemed to penetrate their assumptions about the world. These students hyperbolically claimed that racism was no longer an issue because of Jesus' sacrifice on the cross or Martin Luther King, Jr.'s civil rights work. They cited Rush Limbaugh as a scholarly source on research papers. And they simply could not or would not ever show an ounce of sympathy for the suffering in the world or in others around them. God's plan, for them, was a safe, middle-class existence, which needed vigilant defense against everything from the "gay agenda" to the "godless liberals" of the world.

Most of my students were still innocently saying hi to random strangers on the Mascot Walk. But despite how some students were at first somewhat apolitical, the culture was shifting toward a more radical right point of view. And my own faith was shifting toward the "godless liberals."

# I'M THE TOKEN ASIAN

For all the enjoyment I got out of teaching at EVU in those early years, I was keenly aware of the fact that being Japanese American presented significant challenges I had to work to overcome. If I wanted to connect with my students, I had to overcome the lazy assumptions they had about Asian American men. I had to reach out to them to find common ground. Granted, every good educator should reach out to students to find connection, but I had to overcome a lot of racist baggage to make this connection happen. Students often expressed surprise that I didn't have an accent. You're not hearing an accent now, right? Right?

For my whole life, I had a tendency to fade into the background or fringes of any room filled with White people. I think I told myself I was being "humble" or "observant" before finding my role or my lane in the setting. Coming to EVU made me realize that my invisibility was only partly my choice. White people were actually just ignoring me. Actually, all non-Asian people were ignoring me, and I decided I would help them recognize me. At the ripe age of thirty, I had experiences and knowledge that I knew could contribute to the culture of EVU, and by golly, I was going to make those contributions. What I didn't know was that by doing so, I would be labeled a "troublemaker." White assumptions about Asian American men are a hell of a drug. Apparently, an Asian American man stepping up to lead or teach is a scary thing for many non-Asians.

On the other hand, let me say here that I recognize my privilege as a male professor that my female colleagues did not and still do not have in evangelical spaces. I never had a student present me with Bible verses about why I shouldn't be allowed to teach men. Many of my women colleagues did. I never got accused of being gay because I pushed back against patriarchal views; yes, evangelicals make that connection. I never got called into the dean's office to answer questions about my relationship status or my views on having children. Many women colleagues did. I don't mean to downplay my experiences, but I never had to deal with misogyny against my very person. But I did fight against it.

It's never easy to find connection to a classroom full of students. Even a straight, cisgender White man has to find ways to connect. Ironically, even with every possible form of privilege evangelical culture bestows upon White men, there were a lot of dudes who were terrible at teaching, and students crucified them on sites like RateMyProfessors.com. It was the alpha male professors who exuded a godly Big Dick Energy (BDE) that students tended to respect and love. Even if you were terrible at teaching, BDE gave some men a lot of grace because students assumed they knew what they were talking about. Perhaps ironically, BDE is basically what popular pastors exude.

As an Asian American man, I couldn't assume any positive assumptions about me. I had so much more to overcome to become a professor students trusted, enjoyed learning from, and connected with.

And I fucking did it (adverb).

And there were days I wish I fucking hadn't.

The more I worked to overcome the racist assumptions of my White students, the more I started to question my own instincts to win White people over by any means necessary—because doing so meant both catering to White supremacy and diminishing my own voice. And the more I recognized my instincts, the more I started to unpack just how fucked up (adjective) many White people were.

I didn't plan to stay for more than a year or two at EVU, hoping to find a permanent spot at one of the local community colleges, but I found myself drawn to the students who reminded me so much of myself at their age. They had real questions as they struggled to reconcile the unreconcilable values of evangelical Christianity and the modern world. In my still-Christian mind, I recognized that living this life of evangelical faith made it tough to be a positive force in the real world, where people actually lived. But through God/Jesus/the Holy Spirit, we could strive for it, and that, to me, was the "good fight."

I quickly established myself as a good professor of Freshman Writing Seminar, and the department gave me more classes, until I was at the maximum allowed. As a progressive Christian, I figured I could make the world a better place by helping these students navigate the complexities of life as Christians, I could correct their shitty views of Asian American people, and I could head off the progress made by the relatively new rise of the angry, fearful conservatives on Fox News or *The Rush Limbaugh Show*.

I got good reviews from the paying customers on the official professor evaluations, even with all the gentle pushing and prodding of students to find their humanity. "Mr. Okamoto really challenged us to think and know what believe as Christians in this class," wrote one student. "Professor Okamoto is a really awesome teacher. He doesn't just teach us, he does so much more than that. He is funny and made me think of a lot this year about different ideas and viewpoints," wrote another.

Knowing what we know in 2022, I almost wish I could go back to the year 2000 and tell that thirty-year-old kid to run. But that would deprive you of hearing this story. Spoiler: it's a happy ending. Eventually.

# 2

# Training Jedis in a Sith Academy

## UC San Diego, 1989–1993

When I was a college student, we had an InterVarsity Christian Fellowship (IVCF) leadership retreat every fall semester where we'd take a weekend and head up to some mountain area for meetings and "renewal." Everyone who has been to a Christian retreat or camp knows that they have to be in mountains. Something about being higher in elevation makes Christians feel closer to their God, who, despite being omnipresent, prefers his meetings to be closer to the sky. At least, that's the assumption about God. We can blame the Moses story for this. The Israelites were so fucking (adverb) annoying that Moses had to climb a mountain to get away from them, and God gave him the tablets with the Ten Commandments, twice, on that mountain. If Moses had just gone into a field or gone for a swim, the entire Christian Camp Industrial Complex might look very different today, and we would likely be talking about how good a swimmer Moses was to swim with two stone tablets in tow. There is even a common term used for these experiences: the *Mountaintop Experience*. Something about the location, the beauty of nature, and the intense programming and experiences make the Mountaintop Experience a time-tested phenomenon at these retreats. I wonder if there are satanic camps in Death Valley who experience the opposite. It's the perfect name too.

As a kid I always felt the rush of euphoria with all the singing of worship songs, the deep prayers, and the group (or mob) mentality of being part of a movement to save the world with Jesus' love. I would wish this feeling could last forever and carry us back down the mountain to our flatlander lives. There was even an assumption that such a high emotional state was actually a reality that could be achieved with strict Christian living. This is how it's supposed to be when we're close to God. "Don't let it die!" we were told. "Keep this going!"

Of course, it never kept going, and it never could. And that made us feel terribly guilty. This guaranteed we'd all be back at camp again. Good business model, really. The message was clear: the spiritual high attained at camp was the goal for everyday life. Anything short of that was a failure of one's faith and commitment to God, and since you fail, you've got to keep coming back. This was one reason I was so fucked (adjective) up in the head during my junior high and high school years. College was the time I started to question those early Sunday school teachings.

At the IVCF retreats, there would always be a "be alone with God" time. We'd be told to go off into the woods or mountains or meadows, or some place natural enough for God to meet us. Obviously, he's not going to meet someone by the dumpsters behind the cafeteria or in the bathroom. Duh. We'd all look for a suitably scenic spot to sit, pray, read the Bible, and wait for God to speak to us. One friend admitted he just went to his room and laid in his bed. He was universally judged for that. It's a wonder he wasn't stoned on the spot.

It goes without saying that God never speaks to people right when they sit down. It takes time to get into the right headspace. We were told to quiet ourselves. Apparently, God's voice is, despite his assumed omnipotence and ability to create the universe and everything in it, terribly quiet. How many people really heard him say, "This is my Son in whom I am well pleased" in the Bible? They were all standing at a river outdoors. You can't tell me everyone there quieted themselves properly. It's just not possible. Fortunately, the authors of the gospels heard it to record it for posterity.

So, we would wait and wait and pray, and sit, and hope God would speak to us with some divine insight into how the year would be, either for IVCF or for us, personally. That was the jackpot. If God told us something important for our own development as a believer, there was nothing greater.

In all the years of doing that, I never heard shit. I sat and prayed, begging God to tell me something, already knowing everyone else was taking notes on all the incredibly significant, life-changing things God wanted them to know and do. I spent hours sitting on rocks, logs, and the ground, listening as hard as I could. Nothing. I had thoughts and self-realizations that I reasoned were God's quiet voice. But I never had anything close to a revelation or an earth-shattering epiphany of change or new insight. And yes, I did often wonder if I had chosen the right spot to sit. I knew I should have sat on that other rock!

We would come together after the hour or three hours, or however long we did this. I would be both jealous and skeptical of my fellow IVCF leaders who clearly "heard" God tell them incredible things. The story arcs were all similar. Long waits, because God would never show up at the beginning of any given time slot. It's just not his style. We were all aware of the problematic nature of expecting God to meet us on our terms, so expecting to sit down and immediately hear God tell us something important would have been presumptuous on our part. But two hours after we sat down? He could make himself known without caving to our limited, finite expectations. I guess giving God two whole hours was ample time for him to work. And he often did for seemingly everyone but me. For them, God would tell them to change majors, get a different roommate, stop masturbating, recommit one's faith, stop drinking, confront homosexual urges, break up with a longtime boyfriend or girlfriend. And so on.

I would watch, feeling jealous and skeptical at the same time, as they made their faces appropriately joyous or contrite, depending on their message from God. Some even claimed to feel led to just pop open their Bibles and start reading at the place they opened. Great revelations followed. I did that once and landed squarely in some boring passage of some list of names in the book of Numbers. I suppose if I had been more creative about it, I could have concocted some nuanced lesson God was trying to teach me about time, or family, or heritage. But it wasn't as cool as being told to switch majors.

Of course I now see the folly of the whole thing. It makes perfect sense now that my projection of God, a White male, ignored me. Even while I still considered myself to be a Christian, I recognized the weak theology of fitting God who is supposedly timeless into even a two-hour window for a rare chance at enlightenment directly from him. It doesn't take an expert in human psychology to see past the "messages" those IVCF leaders received from God. The whole thing became a huge part of my deconstruction. What the hell is the point of prayer? Especially the kind of prayer where we ask for things.

# I Think God Wants Me to Stop Going to Church

God apparently "spoke" to people regularly at EVU when I was there. Students would invoke God speaking to them all the time. They would casually declare all the things they were sure God and/or Jesus wanted for them. Some memorable remarks that I thought were contrary to biblical teachings:

"God wants us to only kiss our spouses."

"Jesus wants us to be happy. We just have to let him bless us."

"God doesn't want us to be Democrats."

"God wants us to be wealthy."

"God doesn't want us to sing with guitars and drums."

"God doesn't want women to have careers."

I could do this all day.

So, how does God communicate these specific ideas of daily living outside of the Bible? Some claim to hear an audible voice. Some say he speaks to our hearts. I wouldn't know, as I was never so fortunate to have the direct line to God that so many claimed.

I bring this up because my students at EVU would often ask for prayer. During the first few years I would say a quick prayer before class started, even taking prayer requests. Some classes shared very little, but most had at least one person who would take most of the time. Before I could get to teaching English, the entire class would hear all about someone's boyfriend troubles, roommate issues, or struggles with faith and doubt.

There is something about evangelical Christianity that makes struggle a status symbol. Someone who is struggling mightily with some kind of sin and confesses it publicly is highly respected. "I'm really struggling with the sin of pride," a student might confess. This was the perfect confession. No tangible evidence. No obvious shameful repercussions. If "pride" was a person's biggest sin, all the other typical sins must be totally under control. No masturbating, cheating, murdering, coveting, homosexual . . . ing for that person. Everyone then makes a sad, understanding face and nods. "Me too," another might say. Not wanting to be outdone, another student might chime in, "It's just so easy to get caught up in pride when we need to just give God all the praise and glory!" Now the "amen"s and "yes, praise him"s come out, and suddenly we're in the middle of a fucking (adjective) chapel or church service. It escalates so quickly.

Eventually I stopped praying in class and just asked if students had prayer requests that people could pray for after class. It was a not-so-slippery slope of realizing the theological problems of a prosperity-gospel–style prayer scenario, all the way to considering prayer requests and class time spent praying to be monumental wastes of time. The fact that many professors at Christian schools spend class time listening to prayer requests and praying disturbed me. Some professors bragged that they spent fifteen minutes of class time in prayer every day. But that's why the students came to schools like EVU.

## Welcome, Parents! (Paying Customers)

After a couple of semesters, I had developed my professorial persona. As a college student, I was a quiet kid, watching and listening, formulating my thoughts. I later put myself and my wife through grad school by teaching elementary and middle school, so I learned to be comfortable in front of a classroom of kids. In truth, being a college professor was easier. At least it was to me. The students come in with a respect for—wait . . . let me start over. At evangelical schools, if you're a straight cis man, students come in with a respect for your position. It's less so for non-White men, but it's still there. Women, particularly single women, have to constantly prove their worth to the students who, at best, are iffy on the whole women teaching men concept and, at worst, blatantly misogynistic.

My persona as an English prof was a composite of my favorite professors from undergrad and grad school with a pinch of Mr. Keating in *Dead Poets Society*. My wife, fascinated by my stories of teaching at EVU, came to visit on a day off, and she was a little weirded out. She said it was strange to see me speaking so confidently. It was almost like I knew what I was doing.

Older veteran professors would confide in me that their student evaluations were not great because they weren't entertaining enough. Beneath the surface of these complaints, which were valid, was a not-so-subtle dig at the millennial generation. The overwhelming opinion among the faculty was that the millennials had come to college, and they wanted to be entertained as well as educated. I was young enough to "get" the ethos of the students, and my mildly edgy sense of humor got easy laughs in class. So I could keep the paying customers entertained with only the occasional student or two getting shocked and offended by something I said. It was quite a balancing act.

Despite everything I did to feel at home in an EVU classroom, the school had one more curveball to throw at me. As if to reinforce the notion that they were paying customers, parents of freshmen were invited to attend events and classes during one week each semester. Yes—attend classes.

Most parents had enough respect for their freshman children and their chosen institution of higher learning to stay away and trust that both their children and the institution were fulfilling their respective missions. But every semester two to ten parents always showed up in my classes, looking excited. I was raised right. I knew how to turn on the professor charm for parents.

In the first couple of years, I enjoyed including the visiting parents in the discussions, making them feel privileged to take part in discussing "deep" or "tough" issues and learning to see differing viewpoints. During one of the parent-visit weeks in my second or third year, I had three moms sit in on a class. They were visibly excited to be sitting in on a real college class, and we were in the middle of learning about argumentation. One of the moms told us she was from Kansas, as she introduced herself, and proclaimed she went to a "really big church."

About halfway through the class, which focused on brainstorming ideas for argumentation in a paper, one of the students was proposing an argument paper on interracial marriages. She was Mexican American and wanted to defend interracial marriages. I pointed out that the paper might not work because no one really had socially acceptable arguments against interracial marriages. Anymore. But, to test out what I assumed would be an easy exercise in academic vetting of thesis ideas, I turned to the class and the moms and asked, rhetorically, if they could think of any arguments against interracial marriages. Kansas mom raised her hand, beaming with excitement. Figuring she would point out the silliness of such a proposition, I nodded in her direction with equal enthusiasm.

"Well," she drawled with a deep breath, looking at the other two moms. "At my church, there was a White woman who married a Black man." She frowned and looked around at the other moms. They frowned and nodded knowingly. "When she got pregnant, she had the hardest time. I mean, she was on bedrest, and she had a lot of pain . . . I just think that's God's way of telling us that we aren't supposed to marry outside of our kind." The other moms nodded solemnly.

Every student in that class had met my wife. My White wife who had visited a couple of weeks earlier. Since I don't write with an Asian accent, you might have forgotten that I'm not White, myself. Right? The son of this Kansas mom was a good, bright kid. He closed his eyes, trying to will his mother to stop talking, it seemed. He shook his head and looked down at the table. The other students sat wide-eyed, looking at me to see my response. I just nodded at them and motioned for them to put their hands down and maybe close their mouths. We didn't need to say anything. At least, I couldn't think of anything to say in the moment. If I had told the mom I was married to a White woman, she would probably have felt awful and embarrassed. She had misunderstood my question as permission for her to share her unfiltered racist views. This could only happen at a place like EVU. Something in my words and phrasing had triggered a response in this woman that said she was in "good company." And being among "good Christian folks" allowed her to say exactly what she thought, likely the same way she felt at her home megachurch, at least out of earshot of the woman who had married a Black man.

I switched to a different student's topic and we moved on, leaving the Kansas mom feeling thrilled to have taken part in a "real college class," while the rest of us couldn't look each other in the eyes. Such was the ugly shame we somehow felt from being in the presence of such overt, if happy, racism.

The following Monday, the poor kid came to class early to apologize for what his mother had said. He hadn't said anything to her, but he felt horrible. He had had trouble sleeping all weekend. I told him it was okay and made light of the situation. I was younger then and wanted people to like me. I knew I was a statistical minority, so like many of the BIPOC professors did to survive and stay sane, I tried to remain cheerful and positive. A good Christian would call it "having grace." Had this happened in the last five years of my time at EVU, things would have likely gotten ugly with me saying something insulting to the poor, bigoted woman. I got pretty jaded and cynical over the years. And during the last few years, I informed the school that parents were no longer welcome in my class because twice, parents had visited my class and then tried to have me fired, once for talking about racism in the South, and once for allowing students to read a story with gay characters in it.

I grew up in a White church, and I had heard plenty of racist things said by children and adults. But it wasn't until the incident with Kansas mom that I realized just how comfortably racists fit into evangelical spaces. I had been let into the White world, and Kansas mom had looked upon me and deemed me to either be "White enough" or just not Black. However she regarded me, I was a representative of EVU, and in her mind, that meant I was perfectly fine with racism. A part of me hoped she was the outlier. As someone clinging to Christian faith, I wanted to believe she was the exception. It would only take a couple more years at EVU to make it crystal clear that she was not the exception. I was.

There were others like me at EVU, but in those early days, I didn't know them yet. My progressive faith, hanging by a thread as it was, made me an outsider. Conservative evangelical Christianity was familiar to me, as I had grown up with it, but life had taken me to UC San Diego and the University of San Francisco where I got my master's in writing. In the 1990s, I had become close friends with people who were gay and trans. I drank in pubs with my classmates and professors. I had attended my gay friends' wedding before gay marriage became a national debate. I was starting to believe Christianity was amenable to social justice and equity. I didn't know if homosexuality was a sin, but I didn't think it mattered. I believed women were equal to men in every way.

EVU, as I saw it, considered my Christianity to be wrong. We read the same Bible and worshipped the same God, but we couldn't have been more different.

From a *Star Wars* perspective, I realized I was teaching Jedis in a Sith academy, with "the Force" being Christianity. Or maybe it was the other way around. To the students, faculty, and administration, I was the Sith Lord, trying to lead their young padawans astray to the dark side. From my view, I was leading the stormtroopers away from fascism and bigotry toward a life of love for everyone.

As someone who grew up as a Christian golden child, a part of me really enjoyed being the scary, dangerous, evil one all of a sudden. As I've said, I got along great with almost all my students. I cared about them and their lives. I wanted them to be better people. But the few who hated me and frowned at everything I said . . . Wow. What a rush.

# God-Honoring Diversity My Ass

Like most colleges and universities, the English department at EVU had a small office for the adjuncts. It had three or four student desks where adjuncts could work between classes. About half of the forty or so Freshman Writing Seminars were taught by adjuncts, so there were usually ten to twelve of us employed at any given time. If you were lucky, you would go to the adjunct office and find an open desk to work at. Most times, you were not so lucky. But I did spend some time in that office, and I got to know some of the other adjuncts.

One fellow adjunct I distinctly remember was Fred White. He had been an undergrad student at EVU in the late eighties and became an adjunct professor of English in the midnineties. He was a tall, stern, Native American man who was not what one might consider "warm and fuzzy." If you actually talked to him, he was a great guy. But in a setting where even the White provost poked fun of the university for looking like a Dutch school for girls, Fred stood out. And he was punished severely for it.

Writing his story in *The American Indian Quarterly* in 2003, Fred White recounts the story we heard about in the English department, but barely talked about. He was reading in his '73 Nova in the overflow lot on the South Campus because the adjunct office was full, when White found himself surrounded by three campus safety officers. They demanded to know what he was doing there and didn't believe him when he told them he was a professor. They pointed out that he didn't have a parking permit, even though it was not required in that particular lot. To compound matters, he had left his wallet at home. While waiting for confirmation from the English department that he was an adjunct professor, White asked the officers why they had accosted him when there were other people reading in their cars who also did not have parking permits. Naturally, there was no answer. The confirmation eventually came back that he was, indeed, a professor, but the officers did not apologize. At all. White wrote about his experience in the school newspaper, and whereas any other school would have been in an uproar, the whole community met the story with a big yawn. Even in our department, only a few of us were outraged. Very few. But nothing was done. Not even suggested. Sad story. Poor Fred. Moving on. To make matters worse for everyone at EVU, a campus safety officer wrote a rebuttal to White's story, saying they were just doing their jobs and were justified in questioning him. There was no apology from anyone. Not the school, not Campus Safety. Our department did nothing to press the matter. Like many shitty situations at EVU, they just waited for it to go away. White eventually left for a full-time teaching job at another school that some in my department ruefully described as "much higher paying." Godspeed, Professor White.

The message of Fred White's story was clear to me. BIPOC people, even in the faculty, were, at best, worth less than our White colleagues, and at worst, were potentially dangerous. This doesn't sound all that shocking to us at the time of my writing this book in 2022. Evangelicals are now equated with White nationalism and QAnon. But coming out of the 1990s into the early 2000s, the fallout from the "colorblind" approach to race and diversity was new. It felt like White evangelicals were patting themselves on the back for saying they wanted "God-honoring diversity," as the EVU slogan proclaimed. But they refused to acknowledge their bigoted assumptions and sins, both past and present.

Back when I first got hired, I told my aunt about my new job at EVU. She scowled and asked if I was sure I wanted to work there. She was a researcher at UC San Diego, and one of her research assistants was a grad student who had attended EVU briefly as an undergrad. He was Mexican American, and he told her a story of why he left the school. He was a freshman living in the dorms, and while returning from a jog, he found himself on the wrong side of a long fence along a field near his building. Instead of going around the long fence, he hopped over it and jogged across the field toward his dorm. After a minute, he heard sirens, and he wondered to himself if his dorm was in a safe neighborhood. As it turned out, a White student in the dorms had seen him hop the fence and called the police. They tackled him, held him on the ground, and accused him of trespassing on private property. He didn't have his ID with him, and it was a long ordeal before they let him go.

The school did improve generally over the next ten years, but it did not improve in the number of racial incidents occurring. At all. The school improved in how it responded to racial incidents, which is to say they actually tried to respond. They eventually established town-hall meetings for students and faculty to talk with the president and administration, and they developed processes and diversity training for faculty and staff. Don't get me wrong; none of those things helped. In fact, they actually made things worse, as you will see. But it was a kind of pathetic "progress" that the school at least acknowledged the problems and pretended to respond.

These may have been well-intentioned steps, but they were ineffective in changing the culture, and they were universally detested and disregarded by the students, faculty, and staff. Everyone had good reason to hate the "diversity" programming and messaging from the school. The conservatives hated it because they were White nationalists wearing either Hollister (students) or polos with corporate-looking EVU logos (faculty). Both outfits I would come to equate with simple pointy white Klan hoods. The progressives hated it because "diversity" in White evangelical spaces only meant White people welcoming non-White people and expecting them to assimilate to Whiteness in exchange for a few worship songs in Spanish, maybe a gospel song, a nod to Martin Luther King Jr., and some halfhearted attempts to talk about racism.

# I Am Officially Done with Church

One of the perks of being hired to teach at a flagship evangelical university is that church folk are duly impressed. So, while I was developing a sinister identity as fifth-column[5] liberal filth at EVU, the church I was attending, my childhood church, took notice and assumed a very different narrative going down: the boy who had gone off to "secular" college and "Jesuit" grad school had returned a learned evangelical man.

I was asked by the head pastor to be part of a team at Lake Avenue Church to develop a biblically based Sunday school curriculum centering on diversity. We spent the first half of 2001 developing a six-week series of lessons with three of us leading the classes though discussions and writing prompts. In late August 2001, we went to one of the dozens of adult Sunday school classes and did the first lesson. It was tough material for the middle-aged White people, but they appreciated what we were teaching. The head pastor read through our curriculum and heard positive feedback from the one Sunday school class, and proclaimed that every Sunday school class would go through this series of classes.

As we were not being paid for all this work, I was not thrilled. I was already teaching a full load of composition and literature classes at EVU and at a community college. My colleagues were a lawyer with young kids and a guy who ran a missionary organization. They were both White, but they were both completely understanding of the problematic racist culture inherent in the evangelical world. The idea of teaching twenty or so six-week courses in all the Sunday school classes was soul-crushing. We wondered how we would do this for more than one hundred and twenty Sundays.

---

5. A group within a country at war who are sympathetic to or working for its enemies. The term was used to describe Japanese Americans to justify incarcerating them during World War II.

And then 9/11.

"Diversity" had been declared by the head pastor as the number one priority of the church in 2001, but that priority was shut down along with all the airports in America. Christianity had already undergone a conservative Republican takeover in the eighties and nineties, but now overwrought patriotism got injected into evangelical sermons and books. Diversity was out, and with it our six-week course. We never even got past that first lesson.

I remember a Christian writer proclaiming that 9/11 ensured that the pews in churches would be full from that point on. So great was the fear, shock, and disorientation of the world that many people turned to churches for comfort and guidance. As we now know, the surge in church attendance did not last.

For me, 9/11 was the end of church. I had seen the prospect of teaching for the foreseeable future at the church I grew up in to be some sign that I belonged in church. Maybe God had finally communicated with me, but once that was gone, I couldn't think of any other reason to stay. I really didn't like most of the people at Lake Avenue. So, in direct disobedience to the EVU contract I signed every semester, I became "unchurched." And it was fucking (adverb) awesome. Sundays were now spent making waffles and playing with my infant son. We didn't worry about staying up late on Saturday nights, giving us one more night for wild, mind-blowing sex, which happened once or twice. This would quickly lead to getting pregnant with our second child, but wow. What a ride.

Even before I stopped going to church, I felt conflicted about how I did my job. I wanted to help students learn to write and enjoy literature, and as a teacher I simply wanted to model being a good human being—to help them find love in and give love to the world. But some of them were impossibly hateful and heartless, glaring at me with flared nostrils every time I pushed them to look at their assumptions about the world.

One of my favorite writers is Gloria Naylor, and our literature textbook featured a chapter from her book *The Women of Brewster Place*. The chapter is about a lesbian couple who live in an urban tenement and their struggles to fit into the judgmental culture of their neighbors. This story and the discussions I led about it became one of the flashpoints of every semester. Just asking eighteen-to-twenty-three-year-old evangelicals to consider how they might treat LGBTQIA neighbors was an ethical litmus test for each of them. Some expressed real empathy and care for the couple in the story. Most were conflicted. They knew Jesus called them to love everyone, including the "least of these" (in their minds), but being . . . homosexual . . . their brains went into a rainbow wheel death spiral of reasoning and bigotry. And then there were those who just folded their arms and either snarled in disgust or smirked, as if to say, "I see what you're doing. You can't make me turn evil. Get thee behind me, Satan." In thirteen years of teaching that story, it was always the same experience.

In my Freshman Writing Seminar classes, I started bringing up topics like how evangelicals respond to homosexuality and gay marriage. I had already been playfully labeled by my colleagues as the "controversial" prof, tackling issues like marijuana legalization and sex before marriage. My colleagues, thankfully, assumed I was being "biblical" in my approach, and I was. But "biblical" can be contrary to "evangelical." The idea of caring for poor people and immigrants might be "biblical," but it sure as hell isn't "evangelical" these days. I was becoming more and more determined to show my students that the very Bible they touted was often contrary to their evangelical values.

So, yeah. I was being biblical. What could possibly go wrong?

I received this email in 2001:

Hi Scott! I was just reminiscing about your class last semester, and I realized that I really miss it. I feel it very appropriate to thank you for opening me up to a side of English and lit that I simply had not seen. I can remember going into freshman writing thinking something along the lines of, "Aaaaaaaaah. This is going to be so boring. I hope it goes by fast." But once we got into it, I started to see that I was truly enjoying myself, as well as the opportunity to explore myself and my ability to put a creative paper together. I HAD FUN WITH IT. Thank you so much for pulling that out of me. You were God's tool in my exploration.

There is something very unique and enlightening about your classroom, and I just want you to know that I truly looked forward to and appreciated it. THANKS FOR BEING REAL. You are quite an inspiration. I hope that one day, if I am a teacher (and chances are, looking at my family history, that I will) that I can be as open and as real and as honest as you were with us. I know that sounds corny, but I'm completely serious. You're not only an excellent teacher but an excellent person with the gift of helping others.

I hope everything's going well with little Ethan, as well as the rest that life is bringing you. Thank you again, Scott. God bless.

So, of course it was just a matter of time before I got into more trouble.

# 3

# The Asian Awakens

## ARCADIA, CALIFORNIA, 1980–1988

I started noticing early on that the God and Jesus I prayed to and worshipped were constantly evolving. As a small child, God was an extension of my parents. He was the grandfatherly authority who was kind and loving and demanding of respect for both him and any other authority. As I got older, he was more like a pastor who was concerned about sex, drugs, and rock 'n' roll. If you're keeping score, my parents and youth pastors also fit those descriptions. By the time I entered my teen years, I was fully indoctrinated into conservative fundamentalism, believing alcohol, sex, and drugs were of the devil and would lead me straight to hell. I was terrified of it all, if morbidly curious at the same time.

In Sunday school, I was taught that gay people were evil and wanted to destroy me, my faith, and all that was good in the world with their moral depravity and lust for . . . whatever sin the pastors and camp speakers could come up with. When the AIDS crisis hit in the late 1980s, it lined up perfectly with the narrative that

God's judgment and wrath had finally come to pass on the depraved homosexuals.

It's so embarrassing to think about those days and who that boy was. Thankfully, the message that we were called to love everyone was also instilled in my simple-minded worldview, so despite being horribly afraid of the gay people out there, I knew it was my job to love them and win them over for Jesus. In my mind, Jesus loved them even as he judged them, but he wanted them to repent and become "good Christians" who were holy and definitely not gay. I was taught that the depravity of gay people was a choice, and that choice was an all-encompassing divider. Because they didn't know God's love, they couldn't possibly form loving, caring relationships because . . . um . . . depravity. Yeah. It's nauseating to even write those words.

# UC SAN DIEGO, 1988

When I met openly gay people at UC San Diego, I was really confused. Many of the people I met were kind, generous, caring people. In a flashpoint of my early deconstruction, I was walking through the student center on my way to get lunch when I saw a classmate waving at me. I walked over to her table, and she introduced me to the other two men next to her. I grabbed my lunch and joined them. My friend told me the two men were the president and vice president of the LGBTQIA club. I froze, mid-bite, my heart pounding. I was sitting, eating lunch with two gay men who seemed . . . perfectly normal. I don't know what I expected the leaders of a gay student organization to look like. No, that's not true. I know what I expected them to look like. But they looked like J.Crew models. Clean-cut, all-American, wholesome even. I calmed down and I told them I was involved with InterVarsity Christian Fellowship. It was their turn to freeze mid-bite. Emboldened by what I figured was the Holy Spirit, I asked them if they would be interested in keeping the conversation going between our two groups. They relaxed a bit, and we talked for a while. I was high on Christian-cred endorphins after that, completely unaware that my faith had been radically and permanently altered.

In my mind, I was planning on how I would bring these people to Jesus, but really, the seeds of deconstruction that were already planted got some water. Once I realized that my "godly" view of gay men had been completely wrong, it was the beginning of the end, really. What else was my godly worldview wrong about? The very notion that something so deeply held, so concretely believed could be so clearly wrong was a gut punch to my faith, causing me to shed some fucked-up views. And when I inhaled some actual truth, it introduced something new to my young, sheltered, stupid mind. It introduced me to my first real sense of humanity.

## White-Centered

During college I started to question the "colorblind" views of race that had been engrained in me by both my parents and my church upbringing. My parents' families survived the incarceration camps of World War II and emerged with the view that being Japanese was a crime in America. So, coupled with a 1980s evangelical ignorance of race and diversity, it made perfect sense that I entered college with a mind colonized by Whiteness. This made it extremely easy for me to be friends with White people. I was subconsciously bowing down to Whiteness as the superior identity, so I was not one to push back against subtle racism. I was fine pushing back against overt racism, especially against Black people. Jackie Robinson was a childhood hero, and I was inspired by his courage in the face of overt racism. But I knew I would never have to face that kind of discrimination. I got "ching chonged" and called "nip" and "jap" occasionally, but it was nothing like what Jackie had to endure. I was accepted by White friends. I had dated White girls. I prided myself in being one of the "good" ones.

Naturally this made me fit in perfectly at EVU at first. But the seeds of awakening had been planted ten years earlier, and they had germinated and were growing roots. Evangelical culture, with its White-centered, conservative bigotry, would be just the bullshit needed to help me grow deep roots into . . . okay, enough with the plant analogy. After a couple of years at EVU, I started to wake the fuck up (preposition?).

By the time I was promoted to a one-year lecturer position at EVU, the discarded collection of Gods and Jesuses was getting out of hand. Homophobic God/Jesus, anti-alcohol God/Jesus, purity culture God/ Jesus, Christian-music-is-a-reasonable-replacement-for-secular-music God/Jesus, and many others were sitting on a bench, nursing their wounds and their egos after being kicked out of the game. So many versions of God and Jesus had come and gone through my life, and I started to wonder if version 14.0 in 2002 would last longer than the current operating systems on my computers. I wasn't hopeful. The best I could hope for was a Windows XP kind of God who lasted surprisingly long but really couldn't do without a serious upgrade eventually. The world was changing, and with it my understanding of it and how I fit into it, particularly as a Japanese American man.

## TOUGH CROWD

In 2001, there were only three or four Asian American professors at EVU that I knew of. The others were full-timers who had been there for several years, and I made it a point to seek them out, hoping to form some kind of community in the nearly all-White faculty. Two of the other three that I reached out to showed zero interest in me, especially when I talked about the Asian American community, which I had only recently been finding (more on that later). One seemed friendly and supportive, and we are still friends to this day. But I was dismayed at the others, who seemed to fall prey to the notion that gathering as a group of Asian American profs would invoke suspicion or fear. They had worked hard to rise in the ranks of their White colleagues, and they wouldn't do anything to make those colleagues question their model-minority status. The other Asian American profs knew each other and were in different departments, but I never saw them sit together at meetings or conferences. They seemed downright uncomfortable when I sat with them.

According to my actor friends in the entertainment industry, there is something known as the "rule of one." In any cast or any scene, really, there can only be one BIPOC person. Apparently, we were pushing it to have three Asian American profs, and my presence, even as a part-timer, might have pushed us over a line of comfort for the skittish White faculty. By the time I became a full-time assistant professor, I definitely pushed myself, and myself alone, over a few uncomfortable thresholds.

But I was just beginning to take the first fateful steps that would keep me at EVU for twelve more years. The chair of the English department called me into his office for a meeting that had nothing to do with me being in trouble—a rare occurrence. He told me he needed to teach some classes that got added at the last minute and wondered if I might want to teach his two Introduction to Literature classes. I was honored, as I knew not many part-timers were allowed to teach this class. I had never taught a non-writing class, and I wondered to myself if I could even teach literature. The chairperson told me I could just use his syllabus to get started and tweak it to my liking after I got a feel for the course. I was in.

Freshman writing classes had been small, fifteen-student workshops in small classrooms. Now I would be teaching thirty-five students in larger rooms, and I had to figure out how to lecture and facilitate learning the finer points of literature. I quickly found that I liked lecturing, using humor and bringing a progressive lens to the human condition to enlighten stagnant conservative minds into realities they otherwise would have never encountered. Writers like Flannery O'Connor with Christian backgrounds and critical views of the Church and race made for tense but productive discussions. The Bible, which was often featured in the literature anthology I used, was often the most challenging to read, forcing students to actually look at what was being said.

I loved having them read the parable of the prodigal son, which they all had heard many times. In it, I surprised them as I showed them an argument for the older son as a victim of bad parenting. The students, when asked to see the story from his point of view, had to admit that the prodigal son was kind of an asshole who got rewarded greatly for his bad behavior while the dutiful older son got nothing except a recognition that he was a good son. If you were the older son, I asked the students, wouldn't you be pissed? Students often told stories of their own parents' inconsistent rewards and punishments among the siblings and how maddening it could be. The final blow of the lecture was this: Now, how would you explain this parable to someone who didn't grow up in church? It's not so easy when viewed through a modern lens of parenting.

In the middle of a lecture, I caught my reflection in the window of a door at the back of the room. I was standing in front of the large classroom, gesturing as I made a point about the texts, and I startled myself. It occurred to me that I actually looked like I knew what I was doing. I was developing a professorial persona in real time, finding a confident voice as I guided students through the nuances and elements of great literature. It was a fucking (adverb) rush. Because the bar for English-prof humor is so low, especially English profs at evangelical schools, it was really easy to get big laughs from most classrooms. I learned from comedian friends that the room could be hot or cold, depending on a lot of variables. One variable I didn't expect: the race of the person at the front of the room. It was naive of me, yes, but I found myself surprised that the assumptions students and colleagues had about Asian American men would affect how I was treated and regarded.

To win over any given room, I learned, there needed to be enough people who saw you as a smart, funny person to create the inertia needed for the whole class to buy in. Whenever I had back-to-back classes, I found out just how true this was. I could say something funny in the first class that killed. Students would be wiping tears from laughing so hard. And then I could deliver the same funny bit the second class and . . . crickets.

Throughout my years, I experienced a strange, delayed response to my humor in some classes. I once said something I thought was brilliantly witty and satirical in an offhand remark in the middle of a lecture that made the entire class bellow with laughter. Flush with comedic success, I delivered the same bit in the exact same way the next class. I allowed myself a half-smile at my words, but the class was silent for what seemed like ages. It was likely a few seconds. I continued with my lecture after I muttered, "Tough crowd," to myself. A solid minute later, a girl in the middle of the class burst out laughing. I smiled with her as the class looked over at her, obviously confused. I mouthed the words *thank you* to her and kept talking about literature. She kept laughing and whispered something to her friend sitting next to her, gesturing wildly as if to say, "Get it?" Her friend started laughing too. The rest of the class seemed irritated, as these two laughed, turned red, and teared up.

After class, they came up to me saying they couldn't understand why no one else thought what I had said was funny. I told them what I had said wasn't that funny, but they disagreed and admitted that what kept them laughing was the idea that I had said something funny that went over everyone's head, as if it didn't compute. They wondered if students at EVU were just "stupid or something." I explained that few people expected an Asian American English professor to be funny, but usually classes laughed at my humor. This was an exception, but not uncommon. BIPOC comics and college professors and Rodney Dangerfield don't get no respect.

Another memorable example happened during an early-morning class. I said something I thought was funny and was met with a room of sleepy faces staring glassy-eyed at me. I shrugged and continued on. Later that day, I was chased down by a student from that class who was laughing hysterically. He said my humorous remark hit him halfway through his next class, and he disrupted the lecture because he couldn't stop laughing. "You know," he said, still laughing, "you are really funny." His words were spoken with the weight of someone experiencing a true *aha!* moment. I said something to the effect of being aware of my humor, and he burst out laughing again. "You kill me, Okamoto!" and he walked off down the Mascot Walk toward his friends. Now I was funny because a White dude saw me as funny. Awesome, dude.

I sense your doubt as you read this. But my anecdotes (and there are many more), coupled with the fact that many students admit that they expected me to have an accent and be more "Asian," tell me that their expectations were very low.

Wait. Are you hearing an accent right now as you read this sentence? Laughter. Love. Luminescence. Did the *L* sounds come out loud and clear? Because I wrote them loud and clear. Remember, I have a mild Southern California accent, so go with that if you haven't already.

Usually, by the end of a semester, I could get my classes laughing with ease. I would joke about their innocence regarding their knowledge of sex. Every time anything remotely sexual came up, I would stop and ask them if they knew what that was. "Oh, I'm sorry, do you guys know what sex is?" I would ask. I joked about the tragic unhipness of those of us in academia. I called out racism. But it was always interesting to see how many weeks it would take to establish that I had a certain wit that could be entertaining. Some classes had a lot of students who knew who I was or had taken me before. Those classes started out like gangbusters, laughing from the first minutes of the first class. But a lot of classes felt like concrete walls for the first days and weeks, leaving me pulling my tie, again, like Rodney Dangerfield. Asians don't get no respect. Also, I never wore a tie.

But I wasn't just honing my comedic timing in those literature classes. I had a passion for literature, and I loved sharing that passion with students. The humor was to keep them awake and engaged in much the same way I remembered youth pastors and camp speakers I liked. And I knew I had to do the song and dance for the young paying customers of EVU if I was to remain in good standing as a paid employee. Those dull-minded kids who felt entitled to be entertained while being educated filled out faculty evaluations that could determine our employment the next semester.

I approached lecturing the same way that I, as a thirteen-year-old kid, approached learning how to shred on guitar. I had to outdo my White counterparts just to remain in the game. I couldn't just know my way around a short story or novel. I had to fucking (adverb) kick ass in ways my White colleagues didn't. So, I became the edgy, hard-truth, funny prof. I knew instinctively that I couldn't just be the well-read and well-spoken prof. I had to be the "out there" and "I'm-gonna-show-you-the-real-world-shit" prof. Teaching English, to me, was a subversive endeavor in the context of today's pop culture. In studying language, writing, and literature, you explore depths of thought and value unseen in pop culture. I tapped into this subversive vibe and proclaimed what we were learning to be "dangerous" and "life-changing."

Of course, hardly anyone cared or paid attention. At the end of the day, most students just wanted to know what was going to be on the test or what they would need to regurgitate on the papers. But enough students bought into my approach to form a sense of community. Many of my former students are friends of mine to this day.

# APASO (Asian Pacific American Student Organization) Is Born

In 2002, after an Introduction to Literature class, two Asian American students approached me as I packed up my things. The two women told me they were starting the first ever Asian American student organization at EVU, which they were calling APASO, the Asian Pacific American Student Organization. They had everything in place to become a full-fledged student group, but they needed a professor to be their faculty adviser. I told them I would be happy to, but I was only a part-time lecturer. I named the other three Asian American profs, but they had already declined the offer. I was kind of pissed. Really? It seemed like such an important first-time endeavor, at least to me. I put aside the fact that I was their fourth and likely final option and told them I would be honored to be their faculty adviser, so long as the student affairs folks said it was okay for a part-timer. The women smiled, handed me a three-ring binder with all my responsibilities, and instructed me to familiarize myself with the rules and guidelines I would have to follow. I was supposed to attend all meetings and oversee the leadership, meeting with them on a regular basis. I was responsible for all content in the meetings and had to ensure it all met with the evangelical values of the school.

It turned out that anyone could be a "faculty" adviser in the school's Multi-Ethnic Programs, which was there to support the ethnic organizations. I found out I was the only faculty to be even remotely involved. No actual faculty members wanted to take on the somewhat intimidating requirements of the job, so other ethnic orgs turned to staff to be their advisers. I would be the only faculty member to be involved in any of the Multi-Ethnic Programs for the next ten years, at a school with a stated commitment to diversity.

I went to my first APASO leadership meeting one night, fighting the awful traffic on the 210 freeway from Pasadena for almost an hour to get there. It was a commute that normally took twenty minutes in the morning. But I was there. I surveyed the living room of the on-campus apartment, feeling a little awkward, and feeling the awkwardness of the students who had never gathered with a professor in such an intimate setting. We sat on the floor and introduced ourselves.

The president was the woman from my class, a serious, no-nonsense person who seemed a natural leader. Her friend who was also in my class seemed to be second-in-command, and then there was an Asian American underclassman; a mixed-race couple, neither of whom were Asian American; and one or two others I don't remember. The meetings were serious. Whenever I attempted humorous remarks, I was met with the frown of the president who would then smile politely and shoot me a disappointed look that said, *Why must you be so immature?* So, I just listened and tried to guide their discussions, giving any thoughts I had.

These leaders had recognized racism against Asian American students at EVU, and their way to address the racism was to educate the campus. They planned to have regular, publicized meetings each week with a speaker who would explain the histories and identities of Asian Americans. There would be pastors, a prof or two, some staff—any Asian American people who were both willing and able to come help us educate the racist student body at EVU.

These students, to their credit, acknowledged the racism in evangelical culture, and this couldn't be said for most Asians at EVU. Most of the Asian students I encountered were just happy to be there and happy to do whatever it took to assimilate to the White culture. I never got far, however, when I tried to ask that first group of APASO kids what had brought them to a space that most Asian students didn't acknowledge. I can only imagine the things said to them by their classmates or professors that pushed them to organize and want to help their world at EVU see them and understand them.

But no one in that group really wanted to dwell on the negative features of racism that needed to be acknowledged. The ethos of the group was to instead give the school a chance to learn and grow from the informative meetings APASO would hold. They figured they could love the school and show grace by giving the community a chance to learn and grow. What they didn't account for was the fact that the school did not give half a fuck (noun) about anything to do with Asian Americans.

Almost no one came to any of the meetings. I remember feeling embarrassed for the people brought in to speak to our group. In addition to the six or seven of us leaders, there would be anywhere from zero to three others. We were basically talking to ourselves. It never occurred to those poor good Christian kids that their earnest mission to educate EVU about their existence was not something that would get any attention. I even offered extra credit to my classes of mostly White kids if they went to an APASO meeting. At the beginning, no one took advantage of that opportunity. Not even the few Asian kids in my classes. It was going to take more than an opportunity to learn about Asian American identity to get more students to the meetings.

At the time, I didn't have the knowledge and language to describe what we were experiencing. I knew, instinctively, that I was seen as an "other" at EVU, and I was hearing plenty of horror stories from BIPOC students about the racist shit said to them all the time by classmates and professors. But my own identity as a Japanese American was still, embarrassingly, being formed. I was in the process of decolonizing the Whiteness of my identity and my mind, but there were still a few outposts in there, holding out. I still tended to give the benefit of the doubt to White people who said shitty things. To me, such shittiness was just a normal part of living in America. Like the APASO kids, there was a part of me that held to the notion that just being there and excelling was enough to win hearts and minds. They would see us eventually, and then everything would be great.

I think about that version of me, progressing as he was, and I want to go back and slap him. Sure, I considered myself a "liberal" Christian.

I was beginning my own development as an antiracist. I had spent the past decade exploring my identity as both a Japanese American and an Asian American in this country, so it was timely for me that a new arts space in our town's Little Tokyo had begun right around the time I started at EVU. It would bring me fully and completely into the man I never knew I wanted to be. And it would be there for me when my time at EVU came to an end.

## THE TUESDAY NIGHT CAFÉ

In 1999, just as I was starting at EVU, traci kato-kiriyama, along with her theater and activist friends, started something they called the Tuesday Night Café. Initially, it was a bi-weekly creative outlet for her theater group, Here and Now, and my cousin Lee's band, Visiting Violette. I grew up with Lee, and we had a musical kinship in addition to our family ties. She invited me to the Tuesday Night Café (TNC) early in that first year of its existence, and even though I grew up in the Los Angeles area—in Pasadena and Arcadia—I was somewhat of a newcomer to LA, having just moved there from San Francisco in 1997. I was intrigued at a scene that was predominantly, if not exclusively, Asian American, and I felt both my old mind rejecting it and my new self yearning for it. The old self believed in spaces not dominated by one group. I saw myself as a bridge between White and, well, not White. It was immature and narcissistic at best. Delusional is more like it. And that's where the newly forming identity comes in. I was realizing that to be inclusive of all people, I needed to have a sense of identity and community from which to be in community with others.

I grew up in 1970s and 80s Arcadia, California, where I started out as one of two Asians in an otherwise all-White school. Raised by my hyperpatriotic parents who were born in Japanese American incarceration camps during World War II, I grew up desperately trying to shed my Japanese heritage in order to fully assimilate into Whiteness.

Somewhere in that sludge of identity being formed, I got it in my head that all-Asian spaces were for the weak. I thought I had to succeed in White spaces to make my mark on this world and achieve something worthwhile. It was both a feeling of superiority over other Asians and a self-loathing of who I was. Sad, right? I don't think I would go back in time to slap that version of me. I would probably just give him a hug. And a stern talking-to.

At my first TNC, I sat with my cousins and her bandmate, Glenn, and watched traci's friends in Here and Now do improv, a poem or two, and just kind of goof around. They all clearly knew each other, and they really enjoyed entertaining themselves and the sparse crowd of fifteen or twenty. Outside of Lee and Glenn, I didn't know anyone, and I felt that pang of wanting to belong, even as I judged the theater group for it being exclusively Asian. Lee tried to introduce me to the gang, telling everyone I was an English professor and musician. People were nice, but I felt the divide between us. I was an outsider they knew nothing about. Lee sang a few songs, accompanied by Glenn, and I went home.

A few weeks later, Lee called me and asked if I could read something at TNC that night. They were a short on performers, so she asked if I had a longer piece to read. I had a memoir essay about trying to play competitive baseball in the San Francisco area, and she said that would be fine. Then she sheepishly asked if I could maybe sing a song or two after I read. Were they really that short of people to perform? They were.

The baseball piece was fine, if too long. I remember hearing Glenn laughing at all the right parts in support of me. I sheepishly put down my pages and picked up my guitar. "And now for my next act . . . " But I really hadn't played my guitar or sung in front of people in six or seven years. I had practiced a couple of my old standby songs, but I was super rusty. I should have just sat down after reading. I think I was on that stage in the courtyard of the East West Players theater for twenty minutes or more. In a group I was hoping to find my way into, I felt I had overstayed my time on that stage, and I was a little embarrassed. I didn't go back until the following season when Lee told me she was performing some new material.

I wasn't much of a TV watcher then, or now for that matter, but I was vaguely aware of one of the former Here and Now members, Keiko Agena, who had just landed a role in a show called *Gilmore Girls*. I wasn't familiar with the show, but I knew how rare it was for Asian Americans to be on big shows or in movies. Tamlyn Tomita, another actor, was a hero and crush of my teen years when she starred in the *The Karate Kid Part II*, but other than *Star Trek*'s George Takei, comedian Margaret Cho, and a few minor actors, I had never known about any famous Asian Americans.

Keiko was the talk of the group, and I heard she was still around for Tuesday Night Café when she wasn't shooting *Gilmore Girls*. I don't think I saw her in those early years, but then again, I had no idea what she looked like. The internet was still in its infancy in the early 2000s, so there weren't many ways to look up celebrities and to understand who was who. When her name was mentioned by people I talked to, I just nodded enthusiastically with everyone else. But the reverence for her in the group is an example of the energy and momentum building in that courtyard where TNC met. More people were coming, and there were new people performing that weren't in the original Here and Now theater group.

I was still known as Lee's cousin, if I was known at all, but I was drawn to the TNC scene as a reprieve from life and work at EVU. At TNC, even then, I felt a sense of belonging as a whole person. I didn't go every week during their April-to-October seasons, but I got there occasionally. I started to get to know a few of the people there, including the woman who everyone seemed to know, traci kato-kiriyama. I don't think she knew my name, but she was gracious enough to talk to me once in a while. I immediately saw her as my future, not so much in the romantic sense, although everyone falls in love with traci. I saw her as my muse and guide to a more solid identity and a future away from EVU. At EVU I knew how to play the part, but I also started to realize that doing so meant downplaying or denying a lot of who I was. This is essentially what a lot of Christianity is: denying the self in favor of Jesus. Whatever the fuck that is supposed to mean, theologically, it's certainly a good way to ensure a repressed and codependent populace.

And that's how I started to see the APASO kids back at EVU in contrast with the community at TNC. The APASO kids had to fight racism, but they did so with their hands tied, and they had very little community. They had to fight using the rules of White evangelicalism, or at least that group did. They couldn't be angry or seen as trying to change the system in any way, lest they be judged as "unchristian." We all knew instinctively that we had to tread lightly or face something even worse than our somewhat invisible, inconsequential lives: there was the threat of White wrath if we were seen as getting out of line. Those kids may have been conservative as fuck, but they knew about things like incarceration camps and anti-Asian bigotry.

So, as APASO struggled to get any traction inside of EVU, I invited them to TNC. The first couple of years of APASO leaders had zero interest in anything that wasn't Christian, so they passed. But a couple of the original group came with me to some early TNCs. I felt I had found a special place where I could see myself through the art, poetry, and music in an extended Asian American community, and I wanted to share it with the APASO kids. As time went on, the divide in my life between EVU and TNC would steadily increase, leaving me with both a tough decision and a beautiful life away from EVU. But there would first be, incredibly, eleven more years of my life being bisected into two identities. I would constantly try to merge the two worlds as my role in each grew in prominence and stature. For me, one of those identities would eventually have to win out, but for the students, EVU's roots in fundamentalist evangelicalism would prove too deep. They would not, for the most part, be able to pull up those roots.

## "I HAVE TO GET OUT OF HERE!"

At the beginning of one of the semesters during this time, I noticed a student in my early-morning Freshman Writing Seminar (FWS), sitting there looking either lost or stoned. She seemed to literally be drooling and staring into space. On the first day of a semester, there is a palpable buzz of excitement, with students meeting new people and trying to impress each other. They wear their best new school clothes and pay extra attention to what the professor says. It doesn't last, of course. By the second week, kids are showing up in sweats or pajamas matching their barely awake faces and half-closed eyes. But this girl looked disheveled and completely out of it. She approached me after the class, eyes glazed and wandering, and mumbled something about how early it was.

I had learned that pretty much anyone could sign up for these freshman classes, and I often had to figure out how to deal with international students who did not speak a lick of English. Technically they weren't supposed to take Freshman Writing Seminar, but the computer registration systems were new, and nothing stopped them from signing up. This student reminded me of the special-needs students I also had had experience with. I made a mental note to contact Student Services sometime that week.

The next week, I realized the student hadn't come to class after the second day, so I asked the class if anyone knew where she was. One woman sheepishly raised her hand and said she was a suitemate and that the missing student might be in trouble. The student twisted her face in disgust as she talked and said her suitemate was constantly having loud sex in her dorm room, kicking out her roommate, and marijuana smoke often billowed out of the door. *Ah*, I thought. She had been stoned. The rest of the class looked shocked and appalled. Some snickered and shook their heads. A few students said, "Ew!"

I was relieved I wouldn't have to sort out a special-needs situation. The kids were technically adults, so if they didn't want to come, it was not my problem. Their families were paying a lot of money for them to be there, and it was up to them how they performed as students.

A few weeks later, the missing student showed up after class. She didn't seem stoned this time, and she apologized for not coming. She explained to me that she was trying to get kicked out of the school. She hated EVU, but her parents were prominent missionaries who demanded she go there because she had a full scholarship.

"I have to get out of here," she said almost in tears. She seemed at her wits' end. All she wanted to do was drop out, move in with her boyfriend, and go to a community college. I told her she was an adult and could drop out, but she just stammered something about her parents.

I never saw her again after that day. Her suitemates said she just disappeared one day, and the school told me she had dropped out.

I bring up this poor student to prep you, the reader, for what's coming in this book. Yes, I'm breaking the fourth wall again, looking right at you. Nice desk. That sandwich looks good. Still no accent, right?

This student had her *Matrix* moment, where she realized it was all a simulation of reality. We who grow up in evangelical culture see it as reality, apart from the secular world. When we leave, we realize we had it backwards. My student had somehow deconstructed her faith and just wanted to run away from her family and from EVU. As screwed up as she appeared to be, I found myself admiring her courage to make a change in her life. A free education was not going to keep her at EVU, where she would have to attend chapels, take Bible classes, and answer to the restrictions in the student handbook about sex, drugs, alcohol, and life. And the way the students talked about her, with such judgment and malice, was heartbreaking to me. This person was clearly hurting and going through a lot, and all these good Christian kids could do was snicker and say, "Ew." Nice.

I thought about that student a lot in the subsequent years. My own faith was clearly fading, and my distaste for narrow-minded, mostly White conservatives with no empathy for the world was grating on me. When I contrasted that with the love and care for the world at TNC, I could feel my worldview shifting.

# BEWARE THE OPEN DOORS

Sometimes after one of my classes ended, I'd find myself in hallways and spaces where I overheard things I couldn't believe I was hearing. One day, as I packed up my things and then entered a long hallway of classrooms, I heard a voice booming, like a preacher in the middle of a sermon. The voice was coming from a larger room with two doors at the back. Both doors were open, so I let my curiosity get the better of me and sat down in the hall next to one of the open doors. What I heard astounded me. From what I gathered, it was an economics class. The professor made mention of certain economic principles with stats and numbers. But goddamn he was giving a fiery sermon. I can't remember exactly what he said, but I was struck at how preachy he was being, underscoring all his talk about money and profit with Bible verses and angry, accusatory proclamations about the world with its godlessness and greed. I'll say this, it was a more exciting lecture on economics than I had ever heard in school. But I sat there wondering how my more secular style of teaching fit with this professor's sermonlike lectures.

I looked left and right down the hallway and noted a few more open doors. I had some time to kill, so I ended up sitting next to a few more. Some just sounded like college classes, including the class of a colleague I knew in the English department. But I was surprised to find that there were a lot of would-be preachers in those classrooms. I hadn't been going to my childhood church for a couple of years at this point, and we were actually trying out a liberal Episcopalian church called All Saints in Pasadena. All through my life growing up in church and looking for churches to attend in my twenties, sermons were my least favorite part. I picked apart the rhetorical strategies pastors used. I shook my head at their simplistic theology. I disagreed completely with their conclusions. And in that hallway, I found myself reacting the same way to my preacher-like colleagues.

Goddamn it felt like I was listening to church. And not the good kind.

But I did have an idea. What if I used some of these rhetorical strategies when I talked about literature? A nice slow build, raising my voice dramatically as I broke down stories and themes, would make lectures more dynamic, and I would be arguing for my values. Antiracism. Feminism. Inclusivity for LGBTQIA people. If this was the vibe the students at EVU responded to, this was the vibe I would use.

This "vibe" would also lead to my undoing at EVU.

For now, though, I really felt like I was building a viable career. Despite my loss of faith, I felt good about my abilities as an English professor and as someone who could help conservative evangelicals expand their minds.

At the time, this was all reassuring since I was now the father of two toddlers, Ethan and Audrey. I dropped them off at nursery school on the way to work each day and picked them up on the way home. I look back at those days when everything seemed to be progressing beautifully. I was rising in the English department, making friends with colleagues, and I was helping grow the school's Multi-Ethnic Programs. My family was growing, and my wife's career as a dentist was blossoming. My community at the Tuesday Night Café was growing and developing into both an arts and activism scene. It felt like everything was coming together.

# 4

# The Personal Is Political, But So Is Faith

## UC San Diego, Revelle Plaza, 1988

Lloyd Bentsen, a Democratic senator from Texas and the vice-presidential candidate with the doomed Michael Dukakis presidential campaign, came to UC San Diego to rally students to vote. As an eighteen-year-old freshman who grew up in church, I knew very little about politics, but I went to hear what he had to say. It was exciting to be so close to a national figure in the heat of a presidential election, and just outside of my dorm room. From what I could tell, he said things that made sense. I don't remember much, but I remember thinking his criticisms of Reagan, if true, sounded valid, and his ideas for America's future sounded normal. The little I did hear about politics from family and church had given me the impression that Democrats were evil, so I was confused.

As I listened with some of my dormmates, I noticed a friend holding a sign for the Republican nominee, George H. W. Bush. He was standing with a large group of White guys in Greek-lettered shirts, and they were, apparently, the Republicans. My first reaction was to go stand by them, since I, too, was a good Republican. My family had proudly voted for Reagan, and I would vote for Bush in a few weeks. But there was something about those guys . . . Yeah—they were fucking (adjective) assholes. Nothing they yelled had any substance. They chanted, "Four more years! Four more years! Four more years!" over and over. They chanted, "Bullshit! Bullshit! Bullshit!" when Bentsen criticized Reagan. And that was all I remember them yelling. I did not go stand with them. I found them to be moronic and embarrassing. I was confused by their behavior, since I had been raised believing that the Republican party was the party of family values and traditions. The idea of debaucherous, racist, misogynist frat boys also being Republican just didn't add up. I had grown up assuming that those kinds of assholes were liberals who had lots of sex and drank a lot. It would soon make perfect sense that conservatives were the assholes who partied and drank and were mean to everyone.

When Clinton won the election four years later, I was eating dinner with some friends and a former high school pastor who had just joined the Navy as a chaplain. We watched the election results and bemoaned the horrible thought that this hick from Arkansas had won. Arkansas!

"Well, there goes the military," our chaplain friend sighed.

"There goes everything!" another friend whined.

And yet, the military did not suffer. Taxes did not skyrocket. The budget got balanced. I was a fan of Clinton within months. He spoke intelligently and evoked compassion. I did not see those qualities in the Republicans of the day. Rush Limbaugh and Newt Gingrich did not fit with my Christian worldview. The moderate Bill Clinton was my gateway drug into a progressive existence. As I grew into my progressive self, I would later learn of the racist shit Clinton said and did, but in 1992, I had no understanding of that.

It is fascinating to see how evangelicals allow politics to lead their theology. I get that there is an intimate relationship between a person's faith and one's politics. Both are directly tied to world-view and values. Fine. I may be solidly agnostic now, but even when I was a devout Christian, I felt that theology should drive a person's politics. Not the other way around. For instance, when I felt abortion, drinking, or homosexuality were sins, I believed so because of what my faith taught me. Naturally, I gravitated toward conservative politics and politicians who held the same views. I remember being confused on other matters of faith, though. The rally at UC San Diego happened long before the term *compassionate conservative* was coined so evangelicals could distance themselves from their dickish conservative broth-ers and sisters who espoused hatred and barbed intolerance toward the poor, other religions, or the LGBTQIA community. And I remember wondering why supposed peace-loving Chris-tians could be so gung-ho about war and bombings during the Reagan and Bush administrations. I wasn't necessarily antiwar, but I wondered how a Christian, in light of all that Jesus taught about love, forgiveness, turning the other cheek, and doing things for the "least of these," could be so fired up about war and bombing their enemies into oblivion. I eventually figured it out.

# I Saw It Coming

When Donald J. Trump won the 2016 election to be president of the United States of America, I was heartbroken along with all the other decent humans in the country. But I was not surprised. At all. I mean, I was surprised Hilary Clinton didn't win, but I was not surprised that America's Christians could support one of the most flawed, unintelli-gent, greedy, sexually predacious assholes who ever lived. And why was

I not surprised? I had worked in the higher-educational branch of those people for fifteen years.

That's right. Being at EVU in the early 2000s gave me a front-row seat to the coming of the era of Trump.

It would be easy to paint the EVU cultural landscape as monolithically Republican, but this would deprive you, the reader, of some of the tragic, theologically contradictory, and delicious nuances found just beneath the tidy "A vote for a Republican is a vote for God" ethos that seems to unite Republican voters in places like EVU. Don't get me wrong, the place is solidly Republican. It's so Republican that when a handful of students and one or two professors express ideas contrary to conservative Republican views, those in the majority feel persecuted. I should explain.

According to surveys done by the school's newspaper, the *EVU Tribune*, 80 percent of students at EVU identified as Republican during the 2004 presidential election. I was curious about my own students, so I took a poll of all of my students during a five-year period (2006 to 2011) and it showed 85 percent of students identifying as Republican. The sample of students is a tricky situation. I had the reputation of being a liberal professor at the school, and so I often attracted some of the more, shall we say, "colorful" students. But I always taught at least two Freshman Writing Seminar classes during a school year, and those younger students were consistently more conservative than their upper-class classmates. Also, it should be noted that very few students identified as Democrats. It was never a clean 85 percent Republican, 15 percent Democrat split. At least half of the 15 percent non-Republicans identified as libertarian (although very few understood what that meant) and some felt being identified as Republican was either not conservative enough or they felt that identifying with any political party was somehow against their faith, even though they voted Republican. In practical terms, I could expect one or two students to identify as Democrat in my freshman-level classes and five or six in my larger survey classes of thirty-five to forty that included students of all levels.

Faculty were harder to pin down. There were certainly a few of us who identified as "liberal" in our politics, but we never felt like we could openly express our ideas. Let's put it this way: the school got grant money and material support from groups like the Koch brothers, the famous conservative billionaires known for funding far-right political groups, politicians, and companies. Several departments sponsored internships at only conservative political organizations and businesses. The sociology department offered internships with the Yes on Prop 8 campaign to outlaw gay marriage, which the school admirably asked them to take down. Only the departments of Global Studies and Social Work had what would have been considered a liberal bent, and that was because they openly professed a mandate to help poor, oppressed, and non-White communities and countries. Those are horrifically liberal endeavors in the evangelical world when not pursued in the context of missionary work.

Now, here is the political paradox or "spotlight theory" dilemma I noticed at EVU. The conservative students chose EVU for a number of reasons, but one of the major reasons students picked EVU was the idea that they would not have to encounter the pesky liberal views that plague most places of higher learning. I had students who chose EVU over University of California schools just to avoid the evil liberal professors and the excessive immorality. So, as soon as one of these students heard a classmate talk about racism or heard a professor challenge the notion that voting Republican is a Christian obligation, they kind of freaked out. It just took seeing or hearing one professor giving a different perspective to make some students think the school was descending into liberal or "Marxist" madness. The "spotlight" may have been small, but it was terrifying, nonetheless.

For a few years between 2012 and 2016 there was a Facebook group where students could post anonymous memes expressing their personal thoughts and ideas. A solid half of these were about sex and homosexuality, both confessing to and damning of. But a second category emerged: the persecuted White conservatives. Yes, students honestly and sincerely felt that this anonymous meme group was the only place to express their White pride and conservative views. At a school completely dominated by White conservative students, conservative faculty, conservative Student Life staff, and a conservative administration, conservative students truly felt threatened by a vocal minority and a few outliers in the faculty. From their view, a chapel speaker talking about global warming or social justice was seen as clear evidence the school was going "full-Marxist."

The English department was known to be fairly liberal in the context of the school. We didn't have direct connections to the Koch brothers; we didn't sponsor internships associated with California's 2008 anti-gay marriage bill, Proposition 8; and we didn't exclusively invite speakers to espouse conservative views. When the Harry Potter controversy erupted in the late 1990s, Christians advocated that reading Harry Potter was somehow dangerous. The contradictory nature of an evangelical approach to literature is a head-spinner. They make the argument, as did many of my students, that the objection to many books is that they don't subscribe to their worldview. Dragons, flying broomsticks, talking spiders, and magic wands just don't exist in this world, as created by God, so it is blasphemous or heretical to imagine such falsehoods actually existing. Talking vegetables in *Veggie Tales* obviously do not apply. But evangelicals also made the argument that the witchcraft was just too real, citing reports that the spells and teachings of the witches were authentic, exposing our good Christian kids to witchcraft, which would lead to worshipping Satan or trying to become witches themselves. So, all at once, they rallied against Harry Potter books by saying it was so far-fetched as to be an insult to God our creator, and on the other hand, it was just too real and could lead children into real witchcraft. The only heads not spinning at the thought of this belong to evangelicals. And assholes.

But the Department of English sided squarely with the world of Hogwarts and Professor Dumbledore. In a journal article in the *Conference on Christianity and Literature*, one of my colleagues made the case for why it was a good thing for Christians to read Harry Potter books. This enraged many students and parents, but we held our ground. The books were read and discussed in the Children's Literature course despite the protests and an uneasy, less-than-supportive administration. Despite the almost universal support for Harry Potter, the department, politically, was mostly conservative, even if my former colleagues would claim to be otherwise. The thing is, they would never claim to be either conservative or liberal.

There was a strange vibe in this evangelical school, perhaps not unlike many others. Faculty members generally did not let others know their political leanings. It was just too dangerous for either side. Everyone knew that real academics can't be fundamentalist or staunchly conservative, but an evangelical also can't be a "liberal." Certainly, at a school like Liberty University or Oral Roberts University, the assumption is that every faculty member is a hardcore conservative. Nothing needs to be declared. It's more agreed that science is a ruse of either Satan or God himself. History is a liberal smear against the true Christian America. Fine. That's how those places roll. But at EVU, there was, at least, the claim and the pantomime of being an actual place of higher learning. This put academic evangelicals in a tough spot. On one hand they had their Bible verses about "*logos*" and loving God with all their "minds." On the other, pursuing actual academics eventually meant they would be infringing on the evangelical code, at least the one that students, parents, and donors follow. Most of my colleagues wanted to be seen as actual academics, though very few were by any outward appearance. Almost no one published in peer-reviewed journals because they either didn't care, weren't held academically accountable, or didn't want to be outed as liberal.

At this, I know there are progressive evangelicals cursing at me (yes, they curse), shouting at the book or screen that there are *lots* of academic, nonconservative evangelicals. To them, I tip my hat. And then I ask them, "Where the fuck were you when I was being beat down at EVU?" I know they were there. They were few, but they were there. But I also know they couldn't speak up because to lay claim to a liberal or academic point of view is to invalidate one's evangelical credentials, just as openly claiming conservative views calls into questions one's academic credentials in the real world.

In one English department meeting during the leadup to the post 9/11 Iraq War in 2002, the department chair suggested we pray for the innocent victims of the coming bombings. In the short discussion and the prayer that followed, several people exhibited their incredible grasp of the English language by saying many things without betraying their political views of the war. If they held in their heart of hearts an unwavering support for George W. Bush and his administration, or if they felt, as I'm sure many of us did, that the whole thing was a misguided sham, they did not utter a single word indicating either view. Just, "Be with the children and their families in this difficult time." I know our department was unique in this way. We were hyper-respectful of each other and did not wish to bring up anything that might divide us. Other departments were known to have throw-down arguments. In any case, I like to think those other less linguistically gifted departments couldn't have stuck the landings of the verbal gymnastics necessary to achieve the uneasy but stable environment we created. I often wondered how much more the department could have accomplished if we had redirected all that brainpower to our mission to teach the English language and its literature. Oh well, the administration would have never allowed it anyway.

# The Vote for God

When the fall semester began in 2004 with a presidential election campaign in full swing, I was thrilled to take my two Freshman Writing Seminars on a critical journey in which we analyzed both candidates fairly and critically. By the time Bush emerged victorious in November, my soul was in tatters and my hope for Christian education dashed. I was done. I planned on finishing my one-year, half-time lecturer contract and moving on.

So here is how it went. My plan, as I said before, was to get students to critique both candidates equally. This wasn't too difficult because Bush had four years of his presidency to account for, and John Kerry had a long tenure as a senator. It was hard to compare the two on their own merit because of the differences in their careers, with Kerry as a Vietnam vet and a lifelong politician. Bush had been the party-animal son of a CIA director and former president. But here is where the lesson lay. The poorly constructed arguments of the positions on both sides were easy pickings for any would-be intellectually curious college student. My freshman troopers loved to shred Kerry on his voting record compared to what he was championing in his stump speeches. Ah, but they were downright unwilling to criticize Bush.

"Do you know that Bush has spent more time on his knees in prayer than any other president?" one student said during class one day. She had had enough discussion.

I wondered if they even kept track of such things and asked how she knew this. She assured me her pastor had said it during a sermon.

Halfway through the semester, another student came to me and asked if she could meet with me after class to discuss something. I figured she was upset at the treatment Bush had gotten from a precious few other students that day. Nope.

This student was informing me that she was leaving EVU. Because of me.

She was a bright student who, like most others, didn't like hearing anything negative about Bush at first. But she had slowly come to a point where she could admit he had made some questionable decisions, like any president, she would say. I counted it a major victory to have her reduce Bush from deity status to simply a great, wonderful president. This particular student was known for saying she loved Bush because he seemed like the world's greatest grandfather.

"Wouldn't you just love to have him as your grandpa?" she asked during one of our class discussions. "Just look at him. Don't you just want to hug him?" And, not surprisingly, most others did. Of course I had to ruin the discussion by applying logic and asking if that meant he was an equally wonderful president of the United States.

So, this student had taken some of the valid criticisms of her would-be grandpa/president and shared some of them with her actual grandparents. This would prove fatal to her tenure at Evangelical University. Her grandparents were paying her tuition, and they decided that she could no longer stay at EVU if her English professor was not campaigning exclusively for George W. Bush, the godliest president that ever was. I'm paraphrasing, but it was something along those lines.

It took a minute to register what she was saying to me. She was transferring to another, more conservative, school because I, her English prof, was not telling my students that they had to vote for Bush in the election.

There was no malice in her voice. She was smiling, telling me the situation, incredibly, as if she were telling me about her summer vacation. My heart pounded as I remembered this was the same student who had said that Christians shouldn't get sad when tragedy strikes around the globe. Earthquake kills thousands? No problem. It's all part of God's perfect plan. War destroys whole towns and kills women and children? Nothing but the peaceful assurance of God's infinite wisdom and timing. I was actually glad she was leaving, because she creeped me out. But I couldn't help but feel some panic that this was the reality of her world. I was the evil, liberal professor from whom her family felt the need to protect her. I was used to taking heat for getting students to think critically, but this was way beyond that.

After she was done telling me she was leaving because of me, she handed me an envelope and asked, also incredibly, if I would write her a recommendation to this tiny conservative Christian college I had never heard of. So, in the span of two minutes, she had informed me that I was deemed too evil for her to continue at EVU, and would I please write her a recommendation to a much holier and Christian institution where the likes of me would not be found. It was precious. It kind of broke my heart.

I knew that this student was not in the majority. I stayed awake at nights hoping she wasn't, anyway. Was this an extreme experience? Absolutely. My colleagues and even other students in the class, in many ways, assured me that it was I who belonged at EVU, and not the likes of her. But, coupled with all the trouble I had been in for the regular, everyday battles I fought at EVU, this fall semester of 2004, in retrospect, signaled the beginning of the end for me. It was beginning to sink in that the complaints of a very few fringe students were worth more to the administration than the majority of actual college students who loved being in my class.

After the November elections, several students felt compelled to pull me aside and confess that they didn't want to, but they felt like they had to vote for George W. Bush.

"I knew Kerry would win California anyway," said one girl in class. "So now I can tell my parents and church friends I voted for Bush."

One student asked if he could talk to me after class. He felt guilty and conflicted. He really didn't like Bush, but he had voted for him. He had spent the evening watching the results and praying that Kerry would win, but he just couldn't figure out how to tell his family if he had indeed voted for him. So he voted for Bush. And it was eating him up inside.

I walked with him down the hallway from class. I didn't say anything at first. I just nodded and listened. I assured him that it was okay, that his vote didn't change anything in the election. He sighed and said, "I hate all of this. I hate politics."

I bought him coffee and tried to cheer him up. I reminded him that we'd be discussing sex, drugs, and rock 'n' roll for the next paper. We were all sick of politics.

He smiled halfheartedly, saying he would normally be cheered by such news. But he was depressed. I remember thinking that it was students like him that I would miss the most when I left EVU.

It would be ten more years before I could miss such students, as my plan got crushed by a sense of obligation to the Multi-Ethnic Programs with its growing ethnic student organizations, and a big promotion at the end of the year.

Whereas the assumption among students and my colleagues was that I was a good conservative Christian when I started teaching at EVU, the leadup to the 2004 election had shifted how I was perceived. It's one thing to be a conservative who attempts to teach the "other side" of things in a writing class with the purpose of helping students figure out ways to combat the evils of liberalism. I had hinted that such was the case when I taught argumentation, and it mostly was. It's just that I often did a little too good a job at presenting the liberal view, particularly when it lined up with the teachings of Jesus. Which it often did.

But the 2004 election and the cultural wars fomented by it, along with Fox News and a rising religious right, shifted the whole national political discourse. Even considering another view became a "liberal" endeavor. "Good" conservatives didn't even engage in such filth. And so, while I did nothing to change my teaching of argumentation in writing, the culture took a big step to the right, leaving my centrist pedagogy looking like liberal thinking.

Even still, it was hilarious watching freshmen come in with such supreme confidence in their views, only to have them suddenly not so sure. One assignment I did for a few of these years was to have students argue the opposite side of the arguments they believed in. So, the most popular paper topics were, naturally, premarital sex and marijuana. They were all taught that dabbling in premarital sex and marijuana were the most heinous sins a good Christian could commit.

Abortion was another one, but I had taken a colleague's advice and not allowed that topic to be discussed because Christian freshmen just couldn't handle it. And they really couldn't. The one year I allowed the topic was a clusterfuck of trite sayings, tears, disgusting pictures downloaded from the fairly new World Wide Web, and not an actual logical argument in sight. I noted how there were never tears when we talked about tragedies around the world with children outside of the womb dying or suffering. Several students chafed at the notion that they should feel bad when bombs destroyed and killed homes, hospitals, schools, or libraries. They took comfort in knowing that God was in control, and that was that. One student was even so annoyed that I had brought up such a story that she yelled out, "What are we supposed to do, cry about it?" She was pissed and full of righteous indignation. I told her she probably should, since even Jesus wept when his friend, Lazarus, died. No response. Just glares all around the room. At me. Not her.

So it was just safer and much easier to talk about sex and drugs. The sex part was hilarious. One year, a woman in class made an audible yelp every time the word *sex* was uttered in any context. This was funny on the first day it happened.

Student: "So when we argue for sex (*yelp*) . . . before marriage, can we write somewhere that we are actually against sex (*yelp*) . . . before marriage?"

After a week of this, we all started to just find synonyms for sex to avoid the interruption. And this woman was proud of her tick because, in her mind, she was so pure that she just couldn't even handle the word *sex*. But we were all sick of it, so one day we all just started saying, "Sex, sex, sex, sex." The student screamed, covered her ears, and ran out of the room. She came back a few minutes later, apparently healed of her affliction. She stopped yelping at the word, but she was definitely in a gloomy mood the rest of the semester. The fact that I had lost all ability to care was an ominous sign to me. EVU was getting to me.

## The Campus Has Changed

By the time the nation was ramping up for the 2004 presidential election, the vibe of the campus had noticeably shifted. When I first walked onto the Mascot Walk in 1998, groups of White students said, "Hi," and, "Blessings!" And while that gave me some friendly cult vibes, I came to miss those loving Christian kids by 2004. Instead of the usual welcoming of "other" or "least of these" folks like me, kids were coming to EVU with some serious xenophobia. You didn't need research data to notice the correlation between the rise of Fox News in the Bush era and the now hostile views of "others" in EVU students. Of course, there were still the conservative, caring kids who came from decent churches, but the overall vibe in my classes had shifted into something much more combative.

And even though it was becoming more common to have students cause me significant grief and many sleepless nights, I was still able to connect with most of them. To be sure, there are probably hundreds of EVU alumni who roll their eyes and shake their heads in moral/spiritual angst if my name is mentioned. But most of my students who gave me the biggest headaches became at least mutually respectful with me. This was big on their part and mine. Yes, I'm bragging here.

Still, perhaps the most inflammatory sentence I ever heard uttered—and there were many—was spoken by a freshman in my Freshman Writing Seminar in fall 2003 during the first week of class. As I outlined the types of papers the students would write, I started to talk about argumentation and the various topics we would talk about. Of course, I mentioned politics and race, but I was interrupted by the boy in the front row, raising his hand excitedly.

"Mexican people are all just lazy," he stated. "I want to write a paper about that."

As disturbing as this statement was, what really troubled me was the nodding heads of several other White students. I kind of froze for a second, unsure if I had really heard the boy say what he said.

A few other students protested.

"You can't say, 'all,'" one girl protested.

"No, really," the boy pressed. "I can prove it."

I immediately looked over to the two Latina women in the back of the class, looking horrified. I had heard anecdotes from the APASO kids and others in the Multi-Ethnic Programs about racist shit said by students or professors that went unaddressed. The students had learned to just take it. Such was the reality of life for BIPOC students, but that day would be different at EVU.

I snapped out of my daze. I stopped everything. I told him that was the most racist and irresponsible statement I had ever heard in a classroom. I really laid into him, telling him that such overgeneralizations are irresponsible academically, and just plain hateful and untrue.

To my surprise, the boy just nodded and said, "Oh. Okay."

I was expecting him to put up more of a fight, so I was both confused and a little ashamed for hitting him so hard, but I wasn't ashamed for defending my Latina students.

I was relatively new to teaching then, but I knew that allowing this discussion to continue was pointless. After ripping the kid a new asshole, I attempted to make a teachable moment out of it, using his words as an example of a logical fallacy. Basically, we learned that day to never try to make a conclusion out of any grouping of people, no matter the intent, hostile or complimentary.

The semester went forward without much more on that note. The kid said a few more crazy things and later identified himself as a Rush Limbaugh fan. The strange thing was that he stayed actively involved in the class discussion for the rest of the semester. I had to admit, the kid had some stones. I remember thinking that if I had been yelled at by a professor when I was a freshman, I wouldn't have uttered another word. For a few years. Still, we went at it a few more times that semester. As time went by, I understood that I didn't need to get so angry at him. I always made it a point to create a safe space for discourse. I even wrote as much in my syllabus. This student was apparently just speaking his ignorance to test it out. Must be nice to be a White guy.

When he was corrected, he took it under consideration and moved on. I had been so stressed out by his earlier statement and the positive reaction by the other students, even in the company of two Hispanic students, that I felt as though I had lost a few years of my life. But my fears that a future Klansman was in our midst were allayed as I figured out he was terrifyingly ignorant, but undaunted in his quest to learn. I was always mindful of the influence he had on others, even though he did not seem aware of it. But whenever he spoke his crazy ideas, the same few other students would nod, as if considering their merit. My follow-up to his words was always aimed toward those students. I figured the kid himself was a lost cause.

After the semester ended, I was exhausted and relieved. While I had often found myself looking forward to whatever the student brought up on any given day, it had taken a toll on my sanity. To my great shock, on the first day of the next semester, there he was, sitting in the first row of one of my Introduction to Literature sections.

I asked him if he had been aware that I was the professor of this section when he registered. He nodded confidently.

"You make me think," he said smiling.

But this student was not the only one who showed up at EVU with completely backward and racist views. I remember thinking that had he said his racist thoughts in a classroom at a public university, he might not be alive today. But his views, while not in the majority (I hoped), represented a significant number of students who came to EVU with the assumption that these views were welcome. Some of the students who didn't agree with him also did not speak up against him. I heard countless stories from minority students who had to endure ridiculously racist conversations, accusations, and jokes with not one person calling the racists out.

Perhaps the most telling evidence of the quiet racist culture at EVU comes from a Latino family. The mother had been an employee in several departments for more than ten years, and her two kids both graduated from EVU. All three of them told me that despite growing up and living just blocks away from EVU's campus, they never encountered overt racism until they came to EVU. Something about the culture of "Christian love" and evangelicalism encouraged and invited racism to EVU. And almost nothing stands in its way when it presents itself.

There were cases where the school, despite its best intentions to promote whatever it understands to be "diversity," taught students quite the opposite.

## MEL GIBSON IS AN OMEN

At this point in 2004, I was six years into my time at Evangelical University, and I was done. I told my classes that I was thinking of quitting. It had become obvious that my style of teaching, my now obviously liberal politics, and my open-ended discussions of theology were not what many of the students wanted. I just wasn't sure how many of the students felt this way.

The fact that it was an election year only elevated the divide between my teaching and the conservative evangelical culture at EVU. George W. Bush, by most accounts, had run the country into the ground: unemployment was at record levels, we were stuck in Iraq and sort of Afghanistan with no end in sight, and the economy was showing signs of the looming financial meltdown. So, naturally, the country elected him again. Nationwide, the debate raged. Should we put Bush back in office to finish the mess, or should we elect John Kerry? But there was no battle at EVU. Confirming the student newspaper poll showing that 80 percent of the students were pro-Bush Republicans, students in my classes were fond of the slogan, "A vote for Bush is a vote for God." So, it was God against the evil, godless Democrat, John Kerry. Even though the nation seemed to be split down the middle with around 62 million voting for Bush and 59 million voting for Kerry, at EVU it was a non-issue. This unwillingness to engage in the issues surrounding the election, even at a university, had become something I just didn't want to be around anymore.

I had already been weakened the previous semester by an experience centered around the release of the Mel Gibson movie *The Passion of the Christ*. Mel himself came to our campus to host a preview screening and Q and A with our school's president. The session was broadcast via the internet to churches around the country. Even before its release, the movie had made headlines for its controversial portrayal of the Jews in the gospels as bloodthirsty murderers and Jesus as classic snuff victim. Mel was being called out for his father's fringe Catholicism, which openly blamed the Jews for the death of Christ. Curious to see what all the fuss was about, I had intended on seeing the movie with some friends when it hit theaters.

But the Monday following the weekend screening, the students in one of my Introduction to Literature classes came in still buzzing from both the movie and the brush with Hollywood royalty. (Mel had not yet begun his infamous fall from grace.) Some students were surprised that I had not gone to the screening. How could I miss something so huge? Was I sick that weekend?

"It's just a movie," I said, smiling.

Immediately, a discussion broke out and the room fractured into two groups. There were those who liked and respected me and wanted to know my perspective. They were in the minority, say about ten. The other twenty-five or so cemented themselves into a unified front of anger and resentment. Why it was any of their business in the first place was the real question we should have been discussing.

One girl raised her hand.

"Professor Okamoto, you have to see this movie," she said earnestly. "I mean, you just can't understand Jesus' suffering and sacrifice until you see this movie."

I was relatively young at this stage of my career. I often said things I regretted when confronted with the less intelligent of student utterances. But I do not regret what I said next.

"Watch me," I said. I explained to the class that I did not need a Mel Gibson movie to explain anything about Jesus. I had reached for the very last threads of faith I had. If these kids were telling me a lifetime of Christian faith was insignificant because I had not yet seen a fucking (adjective) movie, then what was even the point of the previous two thousand years? I put my last chips on the table, and even though there weren't many of them left, I was all in.

I could feel the anger and hatred piercing me through frowns and narrowed eyes. So I tried to offer an olive branch. I told them that I would take their lives lived for Jesus in peace and love over a movie any day of the week. I told them that the movie would be languishing on back shelves at Blockbuster in a few months, but their lives would continue to be a positive influence on the world long after the memory of this movie faded. The movie, I was sure, was all well and good, but I'd take their lives over it any day. I took a breath, feeling both the significance of what I had just said, and feeling I had made my point.

At the end of the semester, one dear student told me that those words touched her deeply and made her really think about her life and her faith, and, apparently, she was not in the majority in that class.

A few days later, my department chair called me into his office. By this time, I had lost count of how many times I had received this invitation. Usually, I was called in to tell my side of an event or discussion that had been reported to the office of the school's president. This time, my department chair had a letter from the campus pastor. It was a response to two female students who had come to him to report their very "unchristian" professor and his/my evil ways.

The students accused me of showing pornography to the class and saying derogatory things about the Mel Gibson movie.

On most days, there were usually a number of valid grievances that could be filed by socially conservative students. I forced them to analyze their faith and make them see other points of view. I often used coarse language in the heat of a moment. The previous times I was in trouble were for actual events or things I had said. This time, I was amazed that two students felt the need to make up two things to say about me. Of all the things I did do that students might find objectionable, here I was being falsely accused of two crimes.

I explained to my department chair that I did not show anything remotely pornographic. The only video clip I had shown in the previous weeks was a few minutes of a Chris Rock bit where he talked about racism. (In another issue to be covered later, several students had pointed out that racism did not exist anymore and that I was alone in my feeling that it did. So, I showed a quick clip of Chris Rock.) And I told my side of the whole Mel Gibson movie discussion.

I went home that day feeling depressed. I knew what I had said, and I was proud of my accomplishments in the classroom at EVU. But the words of two students had made the campus pastor hate me. It had been so easy for him to believe them that he wrote a scathing letter to my department chair calling into question my hiring and validity as a professor at the school. It didn't matter what the truth was. He believed the accusations.

My department chair supported me completely. He wrote back to the campus pastor, citing Bible verses about false testimony and pointing out that the students had not contacted the professor in question: me. I was not being given the chance to speak for myself, and that, my department chair shot back, was not a valid way to address the situation. Still, despite the unequivocal support of my department, it felt as though something bigger was at work here.

I read the letters by both the anonymous students and the campus pastor to all my classes the next day. I apologized for offending anyone, but I denounced the accusations as hollow and false. Even the students who didn't like me acknowledged that the accusations were not valid. I said something about considering leaving EVU if my views and style of teaching were not wanted.

"If this is how students and the campus pastor feel, then I guess I don't belong here," I said solemnly.

The classroom exploded into shouts and cries. Some of the students on my side usually sat in the front row, and they turned around in their seats to help me fend off the attacks. But I noticed a face staring at me from the middle. It was none other than the young man who had claimed "all Mexicans are lazy" the previous semester. We had forged a civil, if combative, relationship since that time, but because this was a large lecture class, I hadn't interacted with him in a couple of weeks. I wondered what he was thinking, but he surprised me by standing up and turning around to the back of the class.

He pointed at the students who hated me and yelled, "This is college! Professor Okamoto is the only professor here who makes me think, and even though I don't agree with his views, he cares and wants us to learn. He's the one who belongs here. He should stay. You all should be the ones who go." I wrote his words down in my notes that day. They still choke me up.

The young man turned back to me and gave me a thumbs up. The rest of my supportive students denounced the anonymous accusers. Some said they would sign a letter supporting me or send emails to the school on my behalf. The outpouring of support made me feel validated to a degree, at least temporarily. This would prove to be a trend for the rest of my time at EVU. What really surprised me were my students who said that although they usually disagreed with me, they valued the experience of being in my class to open their minds to different perspectives. There were, it seemed, actual college students at EVU. I'm always happy when students like me. But to me, having students respect my point of view, even when they didn't always agree with it, was more gratifying than anything else. Granted, these students were few and far between, but it was just nice to know they were there.

It did not escape my notice that someone I once assumed was potentially one of my worst students ever became an integral part of the reason I stayed at EVU for as long as I did. And I'll never forgive him for that.

It struck me that the culture I was confronting had sent an ominous message to me. Facts and truth were fine at a place like EVU, but they could never fully eradicate a passionately embraced idea, namely that I was a bad, evil professor, capable of committing unspeakable atrocities in the classroom. For the rest of his tenure at EVU, the campus pastor would speak ill of me to students in his Bible studies and leadership groups. In his mind, I was the face of the evil, liberal professor. Even when some of my students would defend me, he would never change his view of me.

One of his disciples was a popular kid and the quarterback of the football team who had taken two of my classes. He was one who didn't always agree with me but respected me as someone who genuinely cared about students. He was in the campus pastor's prestigious discipleship group and defended me when the campus pastor went off on me. My student told him he didn't really know me and that I was not the person he made me out to be, and he lamented to me that no matter what he said, the campus pastor would not believe anything good said about me. In his mind, the word of two students and his assumptions about an Asian American liberal trumped all else. My boss, the star quarterback, and many others who knew me could not change his view, so I figured I would give it a try. I was getting tired of hearing everything this pastor—yes, a pastor—was saying about me.

The week after clearing things up with my classes, who generally rallied behind me, I wrote the campus pastor a long email detailing my approach in the classroom, my love for the students, and my commitment to their development as Christian thinkers. I even offered to buy him a cup of coffee to help clear everything up. He never wrote back. In all, my department chair, the quarterback of the football team, several students, and I all wrote to him asking him to meet with me to clear up the misunderstanding. He left a year later, never having shared a single word with me in person. I remember being in one meeting where he was present, but we never exchanged words. I didn't think he even knew what I looked like until one event where I saw him and approached him. He turned and walked away, pretending he didn't notice me. There were still only a handful of Asian American men teaching at EVU at the time. He knew who I was. And I knew he was just another bigoted, fucking (adjective) asshole. But I also knew he was the one in good standing, no matter what, and I was the suspect, immigrant, bad guy.

# ANGELS COME TO EVU

Once I started teaching the Introduction to Literature class every semester, I found teaching, in general, to be extremely satisfying. In Freshman Writing Seminar I was teaching writing and argumentation.

In Intro to Lit I was teaching—no, I was evangelizing the good news of literature. I felt great going to work to teach young people critical thinking and the joys and insights of great literature. If only it hadn't been at EVU.

At the same time, I also started going to more Tuesday Night Cafés. The scene was really developing into a place of art and activism, and the focus on Asian American identity in community with all communities felt incredible compared to the White-centered world of EVU.

It was around this time I started a tradition in Intro to Lit that I kept up until I left. Inspired by the vibe of the Tuesday Night Café, I required all students to write a poem and recite it at the end of the semester. It wasn't graded, but they had to do this to pass the class. It was always a great couple of days at the end of the semester when students walked to the front of the room and read their poems. For many, it was a transformative experience, as they wrote about tragedies, victories, or just simple life observations. There were laughs, tears, and snaps.

Since I was regularly seeing my cousin Lee Takasugi, who had brought me in to the Tuesday Night Café scene, I invited her to come to my two literature classes to talk about the creative process to inspire students to write their poems. Her band, Visiting Violette, had made a record in 2002, and her song "On Mars" had won some local awards. It was a beautiful, sad song about the Japanese incarceration camps of World War II. I had the students read the lyrics, and then Lee came in to talk about how she wrote them. It was an amazing success. The students loved Lee and her artful, worldly spirit. On the student evaluations, several students joked that she should be the professor instead of me. I think they were joking, anyway.

It was Lee who told me I should invite traci kato-kiriyama, the founder of the Tuesday Night Café and a poet and writer. Lee told me traci had visited college classes a lot in recent years, but I was hesitant. I didn't know traci at all. She was dating a friend of mine at the time, but outside of that, I had never talked to her at length. But I called my friend the next semester, and he agreed to ask her for me. We ended up talking on the phone, and she was gracious and enthusiastic about coming.

Something inside me was shifting. I was getting to know more people at the Tuesday Night Café, and now I was actually talking to someone I really looked up to. Traci was a hero of mine. Her work as an actress and writer inspired me. My cousin Lee was another hero of mine. The fact that two of the most badass artists in my community would become part of my experience at EVU blew my mind. EVU was where any spirit of art or creativity was smothered in sterile Whiteness and puritanical censorship, and Lee and traci were full-color, high-resolution, beautiful souls with so much life and creative energy that infected everyone around them.

I was going to write that I had no idea traci would eventually become one of the most important people in my life, who would play a significant role in my deconstruction and eventual departure from EVU—someone who, to this day, is a kind of cosmic soulmate. But when I hung up the phone after making the plans for her to come to my classes, goddamnit, I knew.

I also knew I didn't believe in God anymore.

And then EVU offered me a full-time position.

# 5

# The Alt-Right Infancy

## LAKE AVENUE CONGREGATIONAL CHURCH, CHRISTMAS EVE SERVICE, 1980

"And now let's turn to the gospel of Luke, chapter two."

## LAKE AVENUE CONGREGATIONAL CHURCH, CHRISTMAS EVE SERVICE, 1981

"And now let's turn to the gospel of Luke, chapter two."

## LAKE AVENUE CONGREGATIONAL CHURCH, CHRISTMAS EVE SERVICE, 1982

"And now let's turn to the gospel of Luke, chapter two."

I started to wonder around this time, at age twelve or thirteen, why every Christmas, we only read from the book of Luke. In my young mind, the four gospels were, well, gospel. They were four accounts of the same stories, each with a different point of view on the same Jesus. Why not read from Matthew or Mark on

Christmas? You know, spread the love around. Why show such favoritism to Luke? So I read the beginnings of Matthew, Mark, and John, and I realized the reason we only read Luke at Christmas is because there are no accounts of Jesus' birth in the other three gospels in the Bible.

This really bothered me. Call it an early seed of my deconstruction, because Christmas was a big deal to me as a Christian. Jesus' birth, I was taught, was the culmination of generations of prophecies in the Old Testament and the crowning moment of his divinity as a human on earth. How could this seminal moment be omitted by the writers of the other gospels? Of course, I put aside any questions because I was a good Christian child of God and such.

A few years later at UC San Diego, we had to take a freshman humanities sequence of courses. One of the infamous professors was Professor Richard Friedman. All Christians knew about him because he had written a book called *Who Wrote the Bible?* In it, he argues that four writers, J, P, E, and D, wrote pretty much the whole Old Testament. The way his argument works out, it conflicted with our traditional view that Moses wrote the first five books—Genesis, Exodus, Leviticus, Numbers, and Deuteronomy—known as the Pentateuch. As you can imagine, we were terrified to take his course, and I was both relieved and a little disappointed when my schedule had me take another professor for that class. I felt taking this class and directly confronting this evil Professor Friedman was like a final Jedi test to face the greatest of nemeses, like Luke facing Vader. I was a little bit jealous of my friends who were in that class, and I constantly asked them how it was going. Did they go to his office hours to talk with him? What was he like? Did his office smell like sulfur? Did fire come out of his eyes?

One friend, who did go to the office hours, surprised me by telling me Dr. Friedman was a polite, friendly man. My friend had tried to challenge him on the views of the Bible's authorship, but, obviously, he couldn't change the mind of a person who had researched the topic so thoroughly. The feeling was that a person simply earned Christian credits for even attempting to defend our traditional, unresearched, unexamined views of the Bible. Satan was a powerful foe, and the ivory tower was in his domain. We "knew" this.

Just a couple of years after that, we had a symposium on the Bible through InterVarsity Christian Fellowship. We made it open to the UCSD campus and coordinated with a few other Christian groups. A professor in the English department, who identified as a Christian, even agreed to be on a panel with me and a few other students to discuss the way we read the Bible. When the topic of authorship came up, I figured I had my silver bullet. I referred to a passage in some gospel where Jesus refers to the writings of Moses. Aha! Jesus said it, so Moses had to have written the Pentateuch. Did anyone want to call Jesus a liar? I thought not. I sat back in my chair and looked out at the room of a few dozen people, my IVCF friends nodding their heads.

The professor then smiled, raised his hand, and said he didn't think Moses wrote the Pentateuch. He said he was a Christian, and he believed the Bible to be a flawed but useful guide to life. He then rattled off several other issues in the Bible where it can't be taken literally or is just plain wrong. My friends and I were stunned. How could someone who claimed to be a Christian say such nonsense? Even if it actually sounded reasonable.

I am ashamed to admit that I wondered, for a moment, if this professor had been influenced by Satan or some demon to say such things. But he was kind and encouraging after the panel. He talked to a few of us and told us there were many ways to be Christians. He even told us he respected our views and wished us well. He thanked us for including him in the program and headed home.

I will always remember his graciousness, and when I became a professor, I modeled my treatment of students, particularly students who disagreed with me, after that professor. When I started teaching at EVU, my faith was already highly evolved in progressive views, so students often said things about the Bible or church that sounded ridiculous to me. And although I wanted to roll my eyes or shoot them down, I reminded myself of that professor's respectful way of disagreeing. I understood that the journey of faith is a constantly evolving process, and that it made no sense to take any theological disagreements personally.

## REDUCTO AD ABSURDUM

In one of my freshman writing classes, there was a group of boys on the soccer team. They were bright, respectful young White men who exuded absolute confidence in their physicality and in their faith. And in their Whiteness, of course. I got to know them a little outside of class, where they seemed to see me as a kind of mentor. One day after class, as I walked to my car, a base model Volkswagen Jetta with a manual five-speed transmission, the boys came running over with several of their teammates. They were on their way to practice at a field on the other end of the parking lot, and they jokingly asked me if I could drive them. All six or seven of them. Since it was just across the parking lot, I agreed, and they stuffed themselves into my little car, half of them hanging out of the windows.

"Is this like a *regular* Jetta?" one of my students asked through the tangle of torsos, arms and legs. I said it was, and he was surprised. He thought professors made a lot of money and drove nice cars. Not at EVU, man.

In class one day, I made an offhand remark about discrepancies in the Bible and how we, as Christians, handle them. One of the soccer players raised his hand. He looked upset and asked if I had said, "discrepancies." I nodded. He shook his head vigorously. There were no discrepancies, he said. The Bible was the "perfect" word of God.

I could feel his panic. He was feeling the same thing I had felt all those years ago at UC San Diego. But now I was at the end of my faith. I had just read Bart Ehrman's first book, *Misquoting Jesus*, a book I recommend to this day. So even though I thought of a dozen or so specific examples of discrepancies in the Bible, I resolved to help this boy through this moment. I told him and the class that plenty of Christians had varying views of the Bible, but these were not deal breakers when it came to the faith. I didn't believe it myself, but I told the class that a person's faith is personal and should be based on one's understanding of Jesus and the gospels. The discrepancies were not the issue, I explained. The themes and ethos of the Bible were what mattered.

The boy kept shaking his head, and his face turned red. He kept repeating, "The Bible is perfect." Someone in the class added that the Bible being perfect didn't have to mean every word was perfect. It was perfect, as it stated, for teaching and guidance. The boy wouldn't back down. I could tell a few others were on his side, looking doubtful and uncomfortable. I knew they would be confronting these issues in their Bible classes, if they hadn't already, so this was a rare example of a moment when I knew the school, at least the Biblical Studies profs, had my back. I would later learn that the administration would definitely agree more with the eighteen-year-old soccer player, but on this day, I had the floor.

Finally, just to get things moving to what we were supposed to be talking about that day, I blurted out an example of a discrepancy between the gospels. One gospel says Jesus rode into Jerusalem the day before Passover. Another says it happened the day of Passover, and still another says the day after Passover. The boy took out his Bible, because of course he had one in his backpack, and started flipping to the accounts of Jesus' crucifixion. I continued teaching while he read and turned pages back and forth. After a few minutes of this, he froze. His hand was still pointing to a page when he looked up at me, a boy destroyed.

I told him not to worry about it. We had the rest of the semester to talk and explore the many complexities of the Bible and Christian living. I even felt a twinge of renewed faith as I suggested he consider this as a topic for the big research paper at the end of the semester. But he said nothing, got up, and walked out the door. One of his teammates gestured toward the door, and I nodded at him to go check on his friend. He grabbed both his bag and his friend's and went to look for him. Neither of them came back that day, and the next class only one of them returned. The young man who needed the Bible to be perfect had dropped out of school.

I heard rumors that the soccer team blamed me for the kid leaving, but the students in my class did not. They saw what had happened. And they would eventually take the required Bible classes that would, in much starker terms, show the same thing I was talking about.

But here's the thing. I know that the anger toward me in this instance was mainly because I am not a White person. So many other professors had little trouble taking their students down the path of demonstrating the fallacy of the traditional evangelical view of the "inerrant" Bible. But I never heard anyone complain about them. (At least not until my 2022 podcast, *Chapel Probation*, recounted that those professors were able to do so, and then the school threatened the entire School of Theology nine years after I left. The soccer player incident happened a good fifteen years before the podcast.) The idea that someone could be angry with me for simply showing an indisputable fact to a student could only mean those people didn't like me already or simply were looking for reasons to not like me. They never had to look very hard. I made the mistake of being born Asian, and I was a progressive-minded professor.

I felt horrible for what had happened. I replayed the whole scene in my head, trying to think of something different I could have said or some other approach I could have taken. Some colleagues assured me that I had done nothing wrong, and that helped. But I couldn't shake the idea that this kid came to EVU with a faith wholly dependent on the idea that the Bible was perfect. If it wasn't—and holy shit is it far from perfect—then the whole faith crumbles.

I was starting to see such cornerstones weren't limited to the Bible. Other students were convinced that sex before marriage was a direct pathway to hell. Some students believed supporting George W. Bush was a biblical life choice and not supporting him was to support Satan. There were so many binaries indicating a person's salvation, and the more time passed, the more resolute students seemed to be about them. When I arrived at EVU just seven years earlier, students seemed to be able to grasp the many denominational and theological differences under the umbrella of their fundamentalist Christianity. But the students of the mid-2000s seemed to come with intractable absolutes about faith and facts. The line between faith and facts, or even faith and politics, had all but disappeared.

As it became clear that evangelicals had adopted Fox News as the Christian news channel, I assigned Al Franken's *Lies and the Lying Liars Who Tell Them: A Fair and Balanced Look at the Right*. I had found it to be a light, funny, satirical critique of Fox News. I told the students at the beginning of each semester that they would find some of the material troubling, but that they should read it and be prepared to discuss how Franken's points made them think and feel about the role of media. If Fox News was considered the conservative and Christian source of news, what did Franken's points mean? I would estimate maybe 10 to 15 percent of my students even cracked the book open. Some came to class to say their parents told them not to read the book. Others said it was the most boring, pointless book they had ever read. Or didn't read.

Undeterred, I took to reading portions of chapters in class to at least generate some discussion. Always, I reminded them that they didn't have to agree with Franken, but they needed to engage in the discourse of media analysis. Some students read the book and got fired up, both in favor of and against Franken's points. Class discussions usually consisted of two to five students talking and asking questions. The others (there were always fifteen in a section) just sat there looking angry. I imagine some were angry for having to sit through a "boring" discussion of lies and distortions being broadcast on cable news's most-watched channel. But there was always someone who expressed a different reason for being miffed at the discussion. These honest students were simply angry at me for showing them a truth they didn't like and didn't have any answers to.

I usually played a video on YouTube of Al Franken during his days as a host for the short-lived *Radio America*, a liberal answer to Fox News. I would show this video as a complement to the chapters on Bill O'Reilly. In the video, Franken shows a clip of O'Reilly slamming then-senator Joe Biden for saying Guantanamo should be closed during an interview with George Stephanopoulos. O'Reilly then gives his own view of the matter, saying there should be an independent commission to determine what to do with Guantanamo. Franken then shows the original interview and shows that O'Reilly had shown a heavily edited version of the interview, omitting the parts where Biden says he doesn't want to say what he thinks about Guantanamo. Biden only says his opinion when pressed by Stephanopoulos and consistently returns to the point that he doesn't want his opinion involved, stressing the importance of an independent commission. Franken basically proves that O'Reilly edited the clip and then takes credit for making the exact point Biden makes in the original interview. It's ridiculously obvious.

I was always amazed at the students' responses to this video. A precious few sat wide-eyed in horror at what they were seeing. Many of these precious few were raised in families who read O'Reilly's books and kept Fox News on all the time. These students were confronting the harsh truth for them that their world was not what they thought it was. In fact, it was filled with lies and hypocrisy. Sadly, these students were few and far between. Some students sat bleary-eyed and uninterested. It was as if I were showing them videos of paint drying.

But the most amusing students were the ones who looked pissed. They folded their arms. They scowled. They shook their heads. And when I would ask them what they thought, they said very little. I would always press them for some response. Say something! Most would just say they didn't like what they were seeing. Not because they were angry at Bill O'Reilly. They were angry at me for showing something that made Bill O'Reilly look bad. Some told me how disrespectful I was being for showing this video and making them read the book. I was wrong for bringing any negative light to what was so clearly to them a godly, well-meaning conservative hero. Some tried to argue philosophically that O'Reilly was "passionate" and sometimes "reckless," but he was a godly man who was coming from the right way of thinking. "He's only human," said more students than I can remember.

My favorite response came from a sullen self-described conservative young man. After watching the video clip, the students were arguing about the significance of catching a major conservative star in a lie. Without me asking, the kid, who usually just sat silently scowling at me, blurted out. "What an asshole!"

Surprised, I asked him if he was calling his hero, Bill O'Reilly, an asshole. Nope. He said Franken was the asshole for doing this video. I made sure we understood what he was saying. He was saying Franken was the asshole because he made a video exposing O'Reilly's dishonesty.

Exactly. The student went on a tirade about how much work it must have been to put the video together, saying anyone who would go to that much trouble to expose Bill O'Reilly was an asshole. Never mind the fact that O'Reilly first went to so much trouble to put Biden's statement out of context in an obvious lie. In the end, we had to just agree that we had different definitions of the label "asshole."

And that's pretty much where most of my classes ended up. Politically, my students had to confront their views and how they lined up with the Bible, or whatever they thought the Bible said. I asked them to go further and look into how those views lined up with basic human decency. In the end, they, the campus pastor at the time, and most of the staff and faculty would not be convinced of anything beyond the fact that I was, in fact, the asshole.

I'm okay with that.

## THEOLOGY EQUALS SELF-PRESERVATION

About halfway through what would be my last semester at EVU, I was sitting on the floor in the hallway outside of my classroom. I wasn't even trying to eavesdrop, but the class ahead of mine hadn't ended, so I listened to the professor in the room across from mine give what sounded like a sermon. He even finished with a prayer. I had no idea what the subject of the course was. Some other students stood next to me in the hallway, and I knew that the professor taught another class after this one, so I asked the students what class they were waiting for. Predictably, this class and the one before it was a Bible class. Upper division.

Next to me, a student walked up and said, "Oh, snap!" His classmate asked what was wrong, and the student said he forgot to finish his paper. I was greatly amused at witnessing this honest moment of panic. As a professor, I sometimes wondered at how sincere students were when they expressed remorse for not having work finished. And since I'm Japanese American and tend to look much younger than my age, I easily passed for a student waiting in the dimly lit hallway, if I was noticed at all.

"Dude, what are you gonna do?" the classmate asked with a laugh.

Before the student could answer, the professor emerged from the classroom, probably to get a drink of water or go to the bathroom between classes.

The student went right to work. He put on a contrite face to approach the professor and told him he didn't have his paper done. The professor asked why. There were a handful of us in the hallway, and even though my own classroom was emptying out across the hall, I, like everyone else, wanted to see how this scene played out. If the paperless student was aware of the audience who knew exactly what he was doing, he didn't seem to care. Oh, to be a White guy.

The student took a deep breath, slumped his shoulders, made a sad face, and went for it. He told the professor he had been having trouble sleeping for the entire semester. He said didn't know why. He had been struggling to keep up, and now his lack of sleep, he emoted, was catching up to him.

The professor nodded, frowning. I figured that he saw through the kid's story and would instruct him on how and when to turn in the paper. But what he did amazed me. He said something along the lines of the "Evil One" using such tactics to hinder followers of Jesus, and that it would take a lot of prayer to fix the problem.

"In fact," the professor said, looking at a few of his students in the hallway, "let's pray right now." He put his hands on the student's shoulders, which I distinctly remembered we had been instructed *not* to do in our workplace sexual harassment workshops, and began to pray loudly. A few of the students in the hallway bowed their heads.

I watched in awe.

The professor prayed against the evil forces keeping his student from getting the sleep he needed. He prayed for a "hedge of protection" against these forces and prayed for nights of deep, restful sleep for his student. I heard a few whispered, "Yes, Lord," and, "Yes, Jesus," prayer reinforcements from the other students lining the hall. At the end, he added a prayer for wisdom for the student to make good choices about taking care of his body. This made me wonder if maybe he really was onto the kid. I'll never know. They all said, "Amen." I managed to close my wide-open mouth before everyone opened their eyes.

As I headed to my classroom, I heard the professor confirm that the student could turn in the paper at the end of the week before he headed toward the bathroom. When the professor was out of sight, the student high-fived his friend. "Yes! That's why I love going to this school! Professors pray for us here."

I remember thinking that a lot of professors also fall for the "attacked by Satan" ruse to excuse late work. I had heard this one a few times. I always wanted to say, "I seriously doubt the evil lord of the netherworld gives half a shit about your freshman writing paper," but I never did. Probably a good thing.

A few things about the prayer incident. As a mildly cynical person, I was inclined to doubt the kid had any sleep issues. We professors heard all manner of excuses for late work, but a student at a Christian school has a lot more options for seeking an excuse. I heard them all.

"I was up really late praying and worshipping. I just couldn't bring myself to stop the Holy Spirit's moving hand."

"I had a meeting for a mission trip."

"We had cheerleader bonding at the beach."

Okay, that last one could be at any school, but it was memorable because I told the student that her coach had not listed the bonding time as one of their requests for allowing an absence. The student was pissed, informing me just how important it was for the cheer squad to bond and get closer to God. God!

By the mid-2000s, I wrote on my syllabus that mission trips and church activities would not be counted as excused absences. The "attack by Satan in the form of insomnia" was a twist on the usual health-related excuse with the added punch of spiritual warfare. Brilliant. By the end of my time at EVU, weary of these discussions, I started just telling students that maybe God was telling them, via all these trials and tribulations, that they weren't supposed to be in school. Why would God make things so impossible if he wanted you to be here? He's giving you all these "signs" to leave and you're not listening! Listen to God! Get out!

This seemed to be the flip side of the "prosperity gospel" concept. According to the prosperity gospel, God rewards his faithful followers with gifts and stuff they want. These things fall under the category of *blessings*. But those super faithful also run the risk of getting the attention of Satan, thus putting them at risk for attack. And if you happen to be Job, God himself fucks (verb) you over in cahoots with Satan. We learn early on that it's best not to overthink that story.

It's no secret that all people who call themselves Christians have to pick and choose which parts of the Bible they follow. The insomnia student knew his Bible well enough. He knew the coded language of today's evangelical, which references certain sets of verses that are popular in today's evangelical/charismatic lexicon. Interestingly, I don't recall the student initially using these words. He just said he was having trouble sleeping. The professor gave him his out by bringing spiritual warfare into the conversation, and the student, to his credit, jumped on it. *Yes. That's what it is! Satan! The Evil One himself has set his sights on me.* This gives the student a lot of spiritual credibility because he is obviously so faithful and pious that Satan himself has seen fit to attack him. The evangelical professor has nothing else to do except join him in his fight. Schoolwork has to take a backseat to spiritual warfare at an evangelical university. Forget the fact that the Department of Theology could spend ten years debating whether spiritual warfare and attacks by Satan actually exist. At a place like EVU, outside of theology classes, there is simply the assumption that Christian pop culture and contemporary "theological" views rule the day.

And "theology" can get you an extension on a paper you forgot to write.

# Two Kinds of Conservatives

Despite my growing reputation for being one of the Marxist liberals at EVU, I always created classroom environments that were inclusive to everyone, including conservatives. Certainly, there have been students I just could not connect with. There was the girl, who, upon hearing my first day speech intended to shoo away fringe conservatives, sent me a long email explaining that she was going to remain in the class so she could show me the error of my thinking. I had said, "If you think Obama is a Nazi or a Muslim, or somehow both, and you are unwilling to listen to facts about the president, this isn't the class for you." We did not get along at all. In fact, the entire class ended up hating her because, despite being half Latina, she was racist, homophobic, and all-around unpleasant. By contrast, many other highly conservative students often found common ground with me.

In fall 2006, I had a class of solidly conservative students, which was not uncommon. But this class was interesting because one student, whom we'll call Corey, was more conservative and more intelligent than the average eighteen-year-old conservative at EVU. Naturally, he and I debated rigorously the many issues of the day, from the relatively new wars in Iraq and Afghanistan to the basic role of government. I always appreciated his consistency and his ability to express his views. He was just as tough on his fellow conservatives as he was with me. During one class, a passionate but much less thoughtful conservative student got angry with me when I brought up views that were critical of the war in Iraq. We had just read or watched something critical of the decision to invade Iraq, and she had had enough. "Hello? We were attacked, people!" She was not alone in thinking the invasion of Iraq was directly linked to the attacks of 9/11. In fact, most of my students held this view. But not my favorite conservative of that semester. Corey cut her off, saying he was as conservative as anyone, obviously, but he knew there was no connection between 9/11 and Saddam Hussein. It was a rare instance where I didn't have to say anything. Other students brought up party line justifications for the war, but he shot them all down. When another student questioned his conservative commitment, I stepped in to defend him. Using facts and logic didn't mean someone wasn't conservative. I pointed out several conservative intellectuals of the day who criticized the current wars. Some didn't like the cost and some, like my student, just didn't see a connection between the 9/11 attacks and Iraq. It was one day where a hardcore conservative and I were on the same side.

On many days after class Corey and I would walk out together and talk about life, even on days we really got into it. We talked about my kids or his relationship troubles or sports. I really enjoyed getting to know him. We developed a mutual respect despite the fact that our politics were so diametrically opposed.

In the years after, this student became part of a conservative movement on campus known as "the Conservative Voice." They had a Facebook group and a website with the purpose of encouraging dialogue with the greater EVU community, which the group felt had become liberal. Laughable as this notion was, the group had a good run of two or three years with a strong presence on campus. They hosted events with speakers and had several nights of debates on topics like immigration and socialism. They even made sure to invite the leaders of the liberal groups on campus to their events. Generally, this was a nice gesture, but it never ended well. The events were mostly talking points thrown about with no actual discourse. If anything, the students on both sides got an early view into the coming political climate leading up to the election of Trump. The chasm was growing between sides, with the conservatives arguing against human rights and the liberals arguing for their right to exist. At some point—not just at EVU, but in America—the very existence of a few liberals somehow became discrimination against the conservative worldview. There were only a handful of us, with a few outspoken professors in the solidly conservative school, but the conservatives felt they were under attack and at risk of being overrun.

Throughout this surge in conservative movements, Corey and I remained friends.

In Corey, I saw a way forward for places like EVU. There had to be an answer in the concept of people from different backgrounds and different ideologies coming together to dialogue and offer emotional support to one another. Between Corey and the student who went from thinking all Mexican people are lazy to being my staunchest supporter, I found a new sense of purpose at EVU. If it were possible to reach hard-core conservatives on a human level, it would be possible to help them be better humans. If it were possible to be both a conservative and a caring, empathetic human at the same time, this was a way to make it happen. If it were possible to replicate these relationships, there could be a future for an evangelical institution of higher learning. If not, I at least found my "catcher in the rye" mission to help a few individuals.

What I could not have imagined was that I was witnessing the budding tendrils of what would become known as the alt-right. The Tea Party would rise up near the end of the Bush era and lead the racist uprising against President Obama, but I had no idea the students I was clashing with were growing into that. I hoped that Corey and a few one-off people who found ways to rethink their perspectives were bell-wethers for a new era. Especially when Obama was elected a few years later, I really believed conservatives could be reached. Like how Luke Skywalker reached his dad, Darth Vader.

Yeah. I was mostly wrong.

Conservatism is a hell of a drug.

One student I felt connected to I just could not be friends with, and not because of anything we said to each other. Don reminded me of Corey. Outspoken and funny, he was not as serious and intellectual as Corey, but he could always be counted on to listen to different views and consider them. Most conservatives at EVU have their assumptions about what they assume to be liberal views and will not take a second to consider their merit. In fact, most freshmen don't really care to engage in any conversations about political or controversial social topics, citing boredom, disinterest, or faith as reasons for their unwillingness to discuss. But Don enjoyed discussing, displaying a willingness, even a need, to understand differing views. I often wondered how he came to such a mature place in his young life. I found out during a heated discussion of health care.

Several years before President Obama passed his Affordable Care Act, known as Obamacare, we watched a segment of Michael Moore's movie *Sicko*. The movie argues that America's health-care industry is deeply flawed because it pits our health directly at odds with the profits of big corporations who provide and manage the medical care. Don, who was usually enthusiastic and argumentative, was strangely quiet throughout the discussion. When students started admitting that our health-care systems were flawed, Don finally spoke up. He stated that despite the system being broken, he would never want a socialized system like they have in England and France. I asked why. None of us were prepared for his answer.

He told us his father was diagnosed with cancer a few years earlier. They took him to a hospital called City of Hope, where the doctors outlined a treatment plan they felt gave him the best chances of survival. City of Hope is one of the leading hospitals in the world for cancer treatment, and the family was hopeful about Don's father's chances. Then came the bad news that his insurance would not cover treatment at City of Hope. He was transferred to an in-network hospital where, according to Don, the doctors were "clowns." They were limited in their training and their technology, and Don's father died shortly thereafter. It was agonizing to watch his father die without ever getting a shot at the best treatments, and he felt the hospital covered by his family's insurance just set him aside to die and didn't even try to treat him.

We sat in silence as Don wiped tears from his eyes. Through my own tears, I noted a few stoic students who showed no emotion. One visibly emotional student pointed out that, despite the socialized medicine, Don's father would have been able to get treated by the specialists in England or France, so wouldn't that mean Don, of all people, should be in favor of socialized medicine?

Don took a deep breath and nodded, as if he was anticipating this question. "I would rather have freedom than have my dad get treated at City of Hope." Another silence, this one quite painful. I didn't want to state the obvious and just say, "Really?" There was no way he meant it. It sounded like a trite conservative talking point made by Rush Limbaugh or Ann Coulter. Years later in the 2012 Republican primaries, an entire audience during a nationally televised debate would chant, "Let him die! Let him die," when the question came up about what to do with a cancer patient who didn't have health insurance. Tough, inhumane talk all too common for today's conservatives. And here, Don, a thoughtful, intelligent conservative had the Republican rubber and road intersect right through his family, and he was forced to choose between ideology and his own father's chances at surviving cancer. From the looks on the faces of the rest of the class, several students honestly and deeply questioned the values of the conservative movement. The fact that such a choice had to exist really hit them hard. They often left my class angry because they had to hear views different from their own that they couldn't refute. That day, they would leave saddened and dazed because of their own views.

One student took another shot at Don's statement before I could stop her. We were all thinking it, anyway, but it seemed cruel to say it out loud. "You don't really mean that, do you?" Don wiped away more tears and took another deep breath. He was nodding for a moment, trying to will himself to say, "Yes." But that word did not, could not, be said. He excused himself for a moment, leaving us feeling the weight of the moment. All the rigorous debates, some fun and in good spirit, some angry and passionate, suddenly seemed trite and meaningless. Here was a flash point of ideology meeting real life and death. And no one that day was going to argue for a conservative point of view of health care, knowing that to do so would be to support the policies and decisions that stripped Don's father of the chance to fight his cancer. I should feel heartened that my students, solidly conservative as they were, had more humanity and thought than the entire audience at a Republican primary debate. Don returned after a minute or two, but he said almost nothing the rest of the semester. And, sadly, like so many other hardcore conservatives who came through my classroom, I never saw or spoke to Don again.

I don't know if it's on my best days or my worst days that I mourn the loss of that relationship. Things these days are pretty fucked (adjective). And I have no patience for today's conservatives who refuse to engage with humanity. But I did miss talking to Don. Part of me still does.

In a kind of epilogue to the Corey story, Corey and I kept in touch sporadically on social media for the next decade or so. He kept developing in his unique conservative views, and I remember being shocked when he told me he had moved to West Hollywood, a gay-friendly, liberal neighborhood about as far, culturally, from EVU as one could get.

In 2020, I got a message from him. He just wrote, "I guess I've changed a lot. Thanks for being there at the beginning." Attached was a picture of Corey in the middle of a diverse crowd, marching in the streets of LA. Corey was smiling and holding a Black Lives Matter sign.

# Traci Takes EVU

Because I taught two early-morning classes, I arranged to have traci, the founder and host of the Tuesday Night Café, stay at a nearby motel so she wouldn't have to make the ridiculous commute for the 7:15 a.m.

class. Traci was such a good sport when I picked her up that morning despite the shitty hotel and lack of sleep. She was doing this for free to help out a fellow educator in the community.

Walking with her through the parking lot up to the classroom, I felt the weight of the moment. My two worlds were coming together.

I had been going to TNC more regularly, marveling at the many Asian American and Pacific Islander voices performing poetry, music, and dance. I found myself, for the first time in my life, fully leaning into my identity as an Asian American man. I mean, I always knew I was Japanese American in predominantly White communities, and I had resolved to just be the token, the "good" one, the one who got the jokes and put people around me at ease. But at TNC, particularly during the middle of the Bush years, the focus was on creating art to disturb the status quo in society. No one was there to apologize for our differences or our lack of proximity to Whiteness. We were there to define ourselves on our own terms.

It couldn't have been more different from the vibe of Asian folks at EVU. The Asian club, APASO, was growing steadily, but it was a constant battle with the leadership to keep pushing for change and an inward look or a celebration of who we were. I figured if anyone could lead them to a better place, it was traci kato-kiriyama. I barely knew her that day, but I made sure to tell her about the fledgling Asian club with hopes that she would find it in her heart to come to a meeting someday. Knowing her as I do today, I laugh at the anxiety I felt bringing traci in to EVU. Of course she would come.

That day, though, she dazzled the mostly White kids in my classes. She talked about identity and art, and she did what I learned she always does: she made them write. She had the students each say their names, row by row, pausing to honor them. Then she made them write down what their names meant or where they came from. She made those kids feel seen and honored just talking about their names. I recognized some of what I had been doing, forging relationships with my students by focusing on our common experiences, but damn, she was so much better at it. The main difference was that I knew very well that I was deviating from the accepted social norms both in terms of my progressive views and my identity. I was not apologizing for or explaining my Japanese American identity, but I was keenly aware of the gaps between me and my students. With traci at the front of the room, the gaps seemed to disappear. As good as I was as a professor, I had to acknowledge that traci connected to people in a way that was uniquely her own. I knew I would follow her wherever she led, and I had a feeling she and the Tuesday Night Café community were my people.

## THE MULTI-ETHNIC PROGRAMS OFFICE

The first time I walked into the Multi-Ethnic Programs (MEP) office was back in 2002 when I dropped off my paperwork to be the faculty adviser for APASO. And it was kind of heartbreaking.

Just past the door, Black students sat along the wall, eating their lunches. Some were sleeping. A couch was filled with even more students piled on the sides and back. It felt like a bomb shelter, and in many ways, it was. This was where the Black students came to escape, for a few precious moments, the oppressive Whiteness outside. I picked my way through the room smiling at the students, recognizing a few of them from my classes. But they did not smile back. They glared at me with looks that said, "What the fuck are you doing here?"

I realized I was an intruder in their safe space. Most of them didn't know who I was, and even though I wasn't White, I was not one of them. Asians often were and still are agents of Whiteness, and even when they aren't, they are often perceived as anti-Black. I had a lot of work to do, and I would need help.

It was around this time that Dr. Joy Hoffman, a Korean trans-racial adoptee, took over as director of the Multi-Ethnic Programs office, and she made great progress in uniting the ethnic organizations in nearly impossible circumstances. It would be tough to bring people of different backgrounds together in the best of circumstances, but in White-centric evangelical spaces . . . well, I don't recommend trying this.

White evangelical spaces all claim to value "diversity," but what Dr. Hoffman found was that diversity at places like EVU does not include Asian, Latino, or LGBTQIA people and to advocate for LGBTQIA inclusion was grounds for firing. But in her short time at EVU, Joy helped to expand the diversity conversation from just Black and White, or Black versus White, to include all ethnic groups. She basically laid the groundwork for the coming revolution in MEP that saw the most unity and the most activism the school would ever know.

# THE LIST

One evening, after an APASO meeting, I was standing out on the Mascot Walk with some students, talking about maybe going out to the Paradise Juice Café for frozen yogurt or boba. A student walking on the other side of the Mascot Walk came running through the darkness toward us. He had been in one of my classes, and he was out of breath when he reached me.

"Are you okay?" he asked.

I told him I was fine. It turned out he had just overheard his father and grandfather talking. His father was on the EVU board of trustees, and his grandfather was the head of the board that year. They were talking about "bad" professors to keep an eye on, and my name had come up. The poor student was legitimately afraid for me. He told me not to do the same assignments in Freshman Writing Seminar anymore. All those "controversial" topics for papers about marijuana, sex before marriage, and gay marriage had to stop. The board was looking for reasons to get rid of me.

I just smiled. It meant the world to me that this student cared about me as a professor. He was a great kid. But at that point, I was ready to go, and the idea of going out in a hail of gunfire like Butch and Sundance seemed a good way to go.

I didn't change a single thing in my FWS sections. Three different board members attended my Introduction to Literature class in the next few years. They all said the same thing, that they were just there on a routine "get to know the professors" visit. I never met anyone else who received such visits. Did they really think I'd not notice the inconsistency? Two of the board members who visited even seemed to enjoy themselves. I was extra funny and poured on the Christian elements of the stories, invoking writers like Flannery O'Connor and Alice Walker to discuss racism in the South and how today's evangelicals should respond. One didn't seem to like what I was saying, and she sat in the front row, glaring at me, as if she were watching me take a dump. But I was on fire that day with the students responding and participating. After the lecture, she just stomped out without a word. I'm assuming she was mad she didn't catch me worshipping Satan or trying to turn the students gay. Good thing she didn't come to the class the previous week. Bwahahah!

I would not hear from the board directly again, but oh boy did I hear from the dean's office for the rest of my days at EVU.

# 6

# There Really Are Angels

After the meeting, as I was packing up my amp and guitar, the
speaker that night walked up to me and put his hand on my shoulder. He complimented me and the other musicians in our little
worship band and pulled me over to the IVCF staffer of our chapter. He was the pastor of a local Vineyard church, which was a
"charismatic" church known for worship services where people
speak in tongues and dance wildly about. He pulled me over to
our chapter leaders, who were friends of mine, and announced
that he loved the worship of our chapter. Then he pointed to me
and declared that I had the gift of worship. I had never actually
heard of such a "gift," but he confirmed his observation by telling
us he had seen an angel of worship on my head as I led.

Everyone within earshot stared at me, their eyes darting up to
the top of my head, and I just stood there, perplexed as fuck. In
truth, it was not a good night, technically speaking. I had shown
up with a stomachache, my amp was acting weird, and I felt like I

107

had just sort of phoned in the worship. I'm sure I and the rest of the band were technically sound because I always loved singing and playing, but I wasn't feeling the "Holy Spirit" the way I usually did. And now this nutty pastor was telling everyone he had seen an angel on my head. I'm pretty sure we all had the same questions. Was the angel on my shoulders, but his/her face was on my head, or was it just a really tiny angel sitting up there? How did the pastor know it was an angel of worship and not just another kind of angel? And why were we all picturing angels who were White? Admit it. You read "angel of worship" and you pictured a White angel. It's okay. I still do. If heaven on earth is the goal of the Lord's Prayer, heaven is definitely a White-centered place. BIPOC angels likely get all the shit jobs. No Asian angels of worship—no way. They are the angels of accounting or engineering. But hey. The reason those clouds don't fall out of the sky is due to Asian angel engineering. I can be proud of that.

If you're not familiar with the evangelical world, it's actually a stylistically diverse group outside of their voting habits. On the fringes of today's evangelicalism is the Pentecostal branch, which includes the "charismatic" scene. Think people dancing like Richard Simmons, shouting gibberish, and possibly barking like dogs. So, while it wasn't common for our IVCF chapter to bring in charismatic pastors, we threw them a bone every year as a nod to the many ways people interpret faith and worship.

This was one discussion among those of us in the IVCF leadership that became a big moment in my deconstruction. We were divided on the issue of charismatic Christians. About half of us thought it was a valid way to express a person's faith, and the other half, which included me, thought it was performative bullshit. We all had our Bible verses to support our points of view, and it struck me that we all had valid biblical arguments. It was my first instance of recognizing the Bible often contradicts itself.

And it really made me wonder about my musical abilities. When people called me a "gifted" musician as a young man, it made sense to attribute this gift to the divine. Both my parents are tone-deaf, and there were no known musicians on any of the branches of the family tree. But music always came easily to me. From playing piano as a small child to winning sophomore, junior, and senior of the year in high school band and musician of the year in my high school, to playing guitar in garage bands, music felt as natural as breathing to me. So, when the Vineyard pastor told me he saw an angel of worship on my head, I wanted to believe him. When a White pastor tells a young man filled with racial self-loathing and delusions of evangelical grandeur that he has the gift of worship with angels mounting his numb, vapid skull, well, that's just too tempting.

But I also knew some basic theology and had a passing knowledge of the Bible, and thank the stars, a healthy power of observation. The White worship angel on my head just didn't add up. Fascinating as it was.

And this meant music was mine.

## I Prayed the Prayer Away

"I have a prayer request," the student said before class began. I thought for a moment, looking at my notes for the day. We didn't have a second to spare if we were going to get through it all.

"Yeah, why don't we start class with prayer anymore?" another student asked.

All fifteen sets of eyes turned to me. I had started the first day of class with a halfhearted prayer, something I had done since I started six years before. It was always a way to put students at ease with something that felt familiar to them and had lately been used to combat the "liberal" label I had acquired. Early on I had given a few minutes of class each day to prayer requests, partly because I wasn't sure I had enough material as a newer professor to last the fifty-five minutes. But some students took the opportunity to go "full church" and give testimonies and offer up long, sermonlike prayers. Within a few years, I had the teaching thing down, and the prayers were limited to once a week. After the 2004 elections I only allowed prayer through the first week or two.

But by 2005 and 2006, I was tired of the gimmick. I lost all care to put students at ease, instead reveling in their discomfort; it became a tool to disorient them in order to put them back together as caring, thinking Christians.

So, I stared back at the students and told them they could pray for each other on their own time. I sent a blank paper around the room and told them to write their prayer requests down. I then asked the young woman who wanted to bring prayer back to Freshman Writing Seminar to be the prayer coordinator who would type out all the requests and send them to everyone. This seemed to satisfy everyone, although some threw me some serious side-eye. But this was how I dealt with prayer in classes that asked for it. I would go on to even flatly tell students that classes were not churches, small group Bible studies, or discipleship groups. I told them the best way to honor God in that classroom was to learn to the best of their abilities. It convinced a few of them.

While I may have entertained the notion of a God who listened to our supplications and deployed angels to answer prayers or make good things happen, the truth was I didn't believe in prayer anymore.

The truth was I had come to EVU not believing in conservative evangelical Christianity anymore.

The truth was the 2004 election, the marriage of Fox News with evangelicalism, and my long journey out of that faith had brought me to this moment.

And the truth was I no longer believed in God, the Bible, or anything Christian.

And as fate would have it, and after teaching as a lecturer for a few years, I had a choice to make with my career. A combination of skyrocketing real estate prices and a growing student population had put EVU in a tough place. Despite its self-given title as a "top-notch" evangelical university, the pay for faculty was among the lowest of all colleges in Southern California. At first, the English department had one opening for a full-time position, and they interviewed a bunch of people, offered the job, and had the offer rejected once the would-be professor found out what the cost of living was measured against a starting salary in the low forty thousands. After a few years, the English department had three openings with the same scenario playing out repeatedly.

Three of us had "lecturer" positions, and since any new full-time hire would mostly be teaching the lower division classes we were teaching, they gave us each one-year, nonrenewable contracts for the 2005–2006 school year. Our contracts, which did not include any benefits, stated we were to do all the shit every other full-timer had to do, contributing to and helping ensure the strength of education there, but we would be fired at the end of the year. Each year for the next five years I was told not to expect a full-time job the following year.

Our new chairperson in the English department had taken me under his wing, giving me opportunities to do consulting work with him at other schools, and he was worried about my long-term employment. He had graduated recently from USC with his doctorate in rhetoric and composition and had friends in the English department there. When a position opened up to teach in the undergrad writing program, he told me to apply. So, I did. The idea of teaching at a real school like USC was both exhilarating and scary. But I applied, got an interview, and did well.

While we were working together on our consulting gig, my EVU chairperson answered his phone and chuckled. He exchanged some jokes with the person on the other end, and finished with, "Well, you're taking a good one from us." He hung up and told me I had gotten the USC job.

At the time, I was teaching at both a community college and EVU. I figured I could drop the community college and do USC and EVU part time. The pay at USC was more than double what I was getting at EVU.

But then I got the full-time offer from EVU. I figured it was a chance to keep building my skills as an English professor and help evangelical kids grow their minds and hearts. So, I took it. Ironically, taking the full-time job would mean a lot less take-home pay, as the community college pay was a lot more than EVU's, but I would have retirement and health benefits. So, I burned the bridge at the community college and turned down the USC job. To this day I sometimes wake up at night and kick myself for this decision.

My chairperson was happy to have me still at EVU, but he constantly reminded me that the following year was not certain. So, each year I kept my name on the community college adjunct list and was offered classes only to turn them down. This went on for three of the five years I had this contract. I was eventually just dropped from the community college's adjunct list. When I left EVU, I tried to reapply and get back in, but they didn't even acknowledge my application. I had accepted classes and turned them down too many times. And for what? I guess writing this book is the answer.

I found myself as a full-time assistant professor at an evangelical school right when I decided I wasn't a Christian anymore. But I had a plan.

Actually, I didn't need a plan. My plan was to just keep doing exactly what I had been doing. I would promote a progressive form of Christianity as a matter of pedagogical conscience, when necessary, and teach my English classes like I would at any other school. EVU is an accredited school, so my job was mainly to teach English. And lead the students to worship Satan, of course.

## Deconstruction Is Just the Beginning

The deconstruction world at the time of this writing in 2022 is just starting to take off. And for most people, either outside of it or within, the story is the process that leads to this point. People lose faith. People leave the church. And they either live happily ever after or they live sinfully ever after. My story is just beginning here. After deciding I was no longer a Christian, I found myself on a path that felt more in touch with my humanity, my race, and my chosen family in community at the Tuesday Night Café. But for now, I was at EVU for the foreseeable future with an eye out for the end. At first, I believed the words of the provost when he hired me that he was happy I had gotten my foot in the door, and that he really hoped I would become a permanent member of the faculty. But after the first year of playing nice and hoping I had found a permanent career opportunity, it quickly became apparent that something had to give. Either I had to alter my identity to fit in and coddle White nationalism and bigotry, or the school had to completely change its identity. We put up a great fight to change the school, but ultimately evangelical culture is an unredeemable entity. It would become clear that if I wanted to stay for the long term, I would have to change, and that was not going to happen. If they wanted me out, they could come and get me, because I was done playing nice.

I do admit a level of deception on my part when I decided to stay at EVU. The assumption for all faculty is that when we sign our contracts, which contain radically fundamentalist beliefs, we supposedly support those beliefs. In reality, very few professors I knew subscribed to all of them, so the fact that I subscribed to almost none didn't seem so bad. I hadn't been active in a church for years at that point, and although I was going with my family to the occasional service at the ultraliberal All Saints Episcopal Church in Pasadena, I knew I was not living in accordance with the faculty handbook. And that was just the tip of the iceberg.

Evangelical culture was changing rapidly in the leadup to the 2008 election, getting angrier and meaner. Even moderate White students were having a hard time. A blonde student from the Bay Area came up to me after class one day and plunked down a folder in front of me. "I'm done," she said. She had come to EVU because it was a Christian school with a good reputation, but she had no idea it was such a "White school." Yes, this White student was unable to deal with the conservative vibe and lack of diversity. The folder contained several applications to state schools, and she wanted me to write letters of recommendation. She told me she was glad to be in my class because she missed being around her Asian friends back home. I tried to tell her the school needed more students like her to help change the culture of ignorance and homogeneity. Wouldn't creating a space filled with enlightened White students like her make it better? She thought about it but ended up transferring at the end of the semester. It was just too much of a sacrifice for her. I understood. The four years of undergrad go by fast. Why waste them in a place you don't feel you belong? Even if you appear to belong.

I was used to writing letters of recommendation for minority students who had endured racism and ignorance to the point of madness. An all-too-common sight for me at the front of the classroom was a student in tears or near tears at his or her wits end. The monotony of stupid questions, feeling invisible, not feeling like he or she belonged always haunted me. So many students told me that my classroom was the only place they felt safe to be themselves, to feel safe from the racism of the living areas and programming of the school. In extreme cases, my class was the only place to feel safe from racist professors and staff. I always tried to convince them to stay and to forge underground communities. Some did. For me, making ignorant conservative people uncomfortable by confronting them and forcing them to confront me had become a survival skill and a source of entertainment. But I had had years of practice and thick skin. And a paycheck, small as it was. The students had a short window of opportunity to have a college experience, and many rightfully wanted a school that matched their worldview.

Those minorities who insulate their hearts and souls to power through and endure four years have to be able to ignore the blatant racism all around them or find a way to fight it without losing their minds. I have countless stories of success and failure at both. Some BIPOC students arrive knowing the landscape but feeling they have crossed over and assimilated to the majority culture. In order to keep this up, they have to face constant reminders that they are not White and still seen as foreigners or as something "other." Those who fight it are doomed to face the wrath of their fellow students, the conservative components of the Student Life staff, and even the administration.

## An EVU Professor Trope

I taught myself how to speak like a pastor while at EVU, and I could thread the needle of being edgy and irreverent while still maintaining a moral, authoritative vibe. When Bill, a recently retired pastor who had just been hired to teach Freshman Writing Seminar, asked if he could sit in on a couple of my classes, I agreed. And when he visited my class, he probably saw something in his own pastoring in my introduction to FWS. So, it's partly my fault he thought he could ever be friends with me. This guy told everyone who would listen, including every class he taught, that he gave his wife permission to go to medical school. Permission. He was the head of the household, and his wife could not make this decision without his blessing. Fuck that noise. When he told me this, he went into a canned sermon about his views of marriage and family, and I later realized this was some kind of pastor reflex on his part. When getting to know someone, the question of what he does for a living and what his wife does inevitably comes up. Naturally, because his wife was more educated and made a great deal more money than he did, he had to assert his lordship over the household, lest anyone think him less masculine. Or less Christian.

As a full-fledged "pinko-commie" who supports "feminazis," two of his favorite labels for liberals, I had nothing to do with my wife Geri's decision to become a dentist other than to support it. She could have done whatever the hell she wanted outside of becoming an assassin or a woman who would submit to someone like Bill.

The thing to know about Bill is that he was a friendly guy, but he was the kind of friendly guy women often felt uncomfortable around. He could be "pastorly" when he greeted you with "blessings" and told you he would pray for you. But he could also be the alpha male and the conversational bully with his references to Fox News personalities, Ann Coulter, or Glenn Beck. He loved Bill O'Reilly. And colleagues and students who were women confided in me that he was creepily flirty with them, often remarking about their clothes or physical appearance.

I spent a lot of time with Bill as a colleague, and I never felt comfortable around him. Whenever he came to the weekly freshman writing instructor meetings, some of the women profs would tell me how uncomfortable he made them. He eventually enrolled in a master's program in composition at a nearby university and often told us how the feminazis in the class made him anxious. He bragged that he could survive being in the presence of feminists, liberals, and gays, and this would become a badge of courage for him. I pictured him cowering in the back of the room, praying to White Jesus for strength to make it through without getting yelled at.

I bring up this particular colleague to simply say he was the one who belonged at EVU. I was not. He was a White former pastor studying to become an English professor. I was a forever Asian immigrant apostate meddling in the long-held traditions of bigotry and fear in evangelical culture. He was the undisputed head of his household over his MD wife and their kids. I was an equal partner with my wife. He was a sexist relic who would have loved to live in the good ole days when men were men and minorities knew their place. He also taught in the Biblical Studies department, and I often saw him walking with the other old White guys, guffawing and back slapping. He fit right in. I never did.

Our last interaction ever came on Facebook shortly after I left EVU. In a thread he started where he misrepresented the teachings of Martin Luther King, Jr. as supporting conservative racism, Bill lectured me about letting go of my anger and my constant fighting against racism. I told him he was a privileged White man to be saying that, and he got pissed in that fragile White man way. He told me he had relatives who were Jewish and some of them lived in Germany during World War II, so he understood racism better than anyone. As he went on he just got angrier and angrier the more we went back and forth, writing in caps with exclamation points, "YOU KNOW NOTHING ABOUT ME! ABSOLUTELY NOTHING!" I noted his anger and suggested he let it go. Never heard from him again. Fuck (verb/command) that guy.

# The Kids Are Not All Right

If Bill was a perfect example of an EVU professor, the Student Life department was a perfect example of the ethos of students at EVU. Every year, Student Life organized a big move-in event. Picture, if you will, hordes of loud White students on the sidewalk with big welcome signs as families drove onto campus to move their students into the dorms. The kids would all have white T-shirts with EVU scrawled onto them in colorful markers, and they would scream, "WOOOOOO! EVU! WOOOOOOO!"

Now, picture what I have seen myself: non-White families fearfully rolling up their windows and locking their doors as crazed White kids yelled at them and climbed on and into their cars.

117

One Black student recalled to me that "screaming White crowds tend to make us nervous." Indeed. Even more, quiet White families were unnerved by the experience. Now, somewhere, high up the chain of Student Life command, a meeting took place, probably twenty or thirty years ago when the school was, for all intents and purposes, completely White. The plan was likely to generate excitement and enthusiasm for this momentous occasion of beginning a college career away from home. And how to do that? A raucous crowd of screaming students to greet families, of course. To be fair, there are no cultural considerations here. At least there are very few isolated ones. This kind of welcome is exactly the right thing to do. Other colleges probably do it. As for me, I remember my first day on the campus of UC San Diego as a quiet, friendly day of meeting people and organizing my room. My resident adviser was a senior who came by to tell us to just keep things under control and he wouldn't hassle us. And he could get us weed if we wanted. Really nice guy. But considering everything EVU says about "God-honoring diversity," it's a little sad that those in charge of Student Life couldn't see that to many American people of color, screaming White kids is not a very welcoming sight. Screaming White kids jumping on top of your family car and thrusting their screaming heads into it is downright scary.

One Asian American student told me, "My dad saw the kids running toward us, screaming and chanting, and he almost turned the car around and drove me back to Northern California."

Once, while listening to students joke and complain about the move-in day tradition, I pointed out that there were a few Asian American and Latino students among the "welcoming committee." Someone shot back that one or two token minorities in a sea of screaming White faces was difficult to see. Point taken.

Even some White students would say the greeting was a bit much. They recognized the good-natured fun of a spirited greeting, but there was an aggression to the whole scene that could feel more like some kind of frenzied hazing than a warm reception filled with enthusiasm at your arrival.

From my view, the Student Life programming and staff had more influence over the lives of the students than the faculty ever did. I'm not just pointing this out to tell interesting stories. Every year, Student Life held a campuswide game called Zombies, or something similar. A few students were designated as zombies to start, and they threw a ball of tape at their victims to turn them into zombies. Good fun. But as the week progressed, students were known to skip chapel and skip classes to avoid being turned into zombies. Some even missed quizzes and tests just to survive the game and possibly win an iPod. Such was the influence of Student Life programming.

And I have to tell yet another story because the image, to me, represents EVU so perfectly. After an Asian club meeting one night, I saw a Black student of mine sprint past me, followed by a mob of White zombie students. They circled the Mascot Walk a couple of times, and when my student ran past me again, he saw me, shrugged, and smiled sheepishly before disappearing into the night with the screaming mob of White boys in hot pursuit.

Most minorities and certainly most of us working with the Multi-Ethnic Programs office would agree that the ethos of the school was upper-middle-class White American, plain and simple. In my mind, I can't, for the life of me, figure out which came first: Did the school's legacy and PR attract students who come from culturally clueless families? Or did the school make students culturally clueless? Actually, I do know what I think. It's both. And it's fucking (adverb) sad.

# THE ASIANS ARE NOT OKAY

There weren't many Asians at EVU during this time. I think we made up about 3 percent of the EVU population in 2005, and my mission to bring a Tuesday Night Café vibe to EVU was going nowhere. I had

Asian and Asian American Pacific Islander (AAPI) students in most of my classes, maybe one or two in each one, and almost none of them were remotely interested in coming to the Asian club, APASO. The idea of exploring an identity so far outside of the White identity could never really take hold of the AAPI kids who came to EVU. For the most part, those kids came to EVU to take their shot at assimilating to and being accepted by Whiteness. Talking about their heritage or the rampant racism at EVU would be a hinderance to this quest, so . . . nope. They did not want to come to APASO.

I even started offering extra credit for students who came to some of the bigger APASO events that addressed identity and racism, and while one or two White students always took advantage of it, almost none of the AAPI students did. Ever.

Sam defied all labels. He was a gregarious, if charismatic (in all senses) boy who forged a persona as a would-be preacher. He took my Intro to Lit class, and he came in on the first day wearing a shirt and a tie. He walked straight up to me and shook my hand, and I was impressed by the seemingly driven and well-spoken young Japanese American male student. Most AAPI students sat in the back and didn't really want to interact with me. In some cases, AAPI students resented me for being outspoken. It was an "old-school" perspective where AAPI people felt like outspoken people were uppity or over-confident. In other cases, AAPI students felt like they had crossed over to Whiteness and me crusading against racism was ruining their hard-won place as "good," gracious Asians who weren't bothered by racism.

Sam took his seat between what appeared to be two popular and attractive White women who greeted him with big hugs and exchanges of Christian greetings. At this, I was not impressed. I knew what I was seeing. There was a type of White woman at EVU who loved to befriend minority males, but they would never date one. What I was seeing was a clearly defined relationship, based not on attraction, at least not on the girls' part, but on a desire to appear to love all God's peoples, platonically, and a deeply held respect for the spiritual leaders among the student population. Honestly, it felt like a version of the straight woman's gay best friend. An emasculated Asian male was a reasonable substitute. It also reminded me of the pictures White women post of their short-term mission trips featuring their White faces in a sea of Black and Brown children.

The problem was, Sam was not so much a spiritual leader. Sure he played or cosplayed one, but this was his angle to have at least brotherly contact with Christian White women. I rarely saw him chatting with other male students. But, since he was a rare Japanese American male, I made it a point to talk to him whenever I could.

Before class one day, I showed pictures of my young family after I booted up my laptop to show some slides I had prepared. Sam chased me down in the parking lot after class.

"How the heck did you do it?" he panted as he caught up to me. I wasn't sure how to answer this question. It was certainly a creepy question, but I knew what he was getting at. I dodged the question and we talked about his struggles to fit in at EVU. Turned out, he knew the score as well as I did. Those girls hugging him and saving a seat for him might as well have been on a different planet when it came to an actual relationship. To them, he was a brotherly, big (Sam was a portly young lad) bear of a Christian . . . entity. Their association with him made them that much more Christian (think "least of these"), and that much less shallow snobs.

Then Sam disappeared for a few weeks. He stopped coming to class and did not turn in a single assignment, nor did he take any of the quizzes or exams. When he did come by, it was to tell me he had some ministry to attend to or some important meeting. I had seen this before. I had, long before, made it a point to explain to students that mission work and church work were not excused absences. I even wrote it in bold on my syllabi.

Sam made his triumphant return to the class a few weeks later and dressed for the occasion. Clad in his preacher attire, he approached me at the beginning of class to tell me that God had been working amazing things in his life. He started to tell me all about it, but I had to cut him off. Class was starting.

He took his seat and immediately raised his hand when I started my lecture on the stories that day. I hesitantly nodded in his direction, and he said something to the effect of, "That's really interesting, and it reminds me of how amazing God is because he forgives us when we do bad things and—"

I cut him off and tried to get back to the story we were discussing, which had nothing to do with forgiveness or God. Sam was undeterred and raised his hand again.

I hesitantly nodded in his direction and asked if he had anything to ask or say about the story.

He said he did and went back to his sermon on God's forgiveness. This was disturbing on many levels, but what really freaked me out was seeing students around the class nodding at the points in his sermon. They were unfazed at a goddamn sermon being preached in the middle of my class, and in a kind of theo-Pavlovian response, fell right into church mode. Someone said, "Amen." I guess the kid really was a preacher after all.

Of course, others were just as disturbed as I, turning in their chairs to see who the hell was acting like a dumbass in the middle of class.

I cut him off the second time. Part of me wanted to see just how far Sam would go. Did he have a full sermon prepared? He wasn't saying anything of substance. It was something along the lines of how broken we are and corrupted with sin to not see how good God is and how great his forgiveness is. Yada, yada, yada.

Sam, upon being cut off, walked to the front of the room where the computer station was. He asked if he could just make one more point. Feeling the absolute bizarre nature of the moment, and already planning on telling this story at a bar someday, I relented. Go right ahead, my man.

Sam took a CD out of his coat pocket and inserted it into the computer, which was connected to the class PA system and big drop-down screen at the front of the room. Worship music flowed from the speakers. For those of you not familiar with this cursed genre, think Yanni or Kenny G ballads with Bible verses for lyrics. The music washed over us with some students, fully caught up in the tent-revival moment, lifting their arms in worship. Most, however, just stared, dumbfounded. I sat down at the desk at the front of the room, put my head on my hands, and tried desperately not to laugh out loud.

Inspired by the music, Sam doubled his efforts and began to sweat as he relaunched into the same message, enunciating every syllable. God is so, so, so very good. We broken, sinful humans sometimes don't take the time to appreciate him.

After a minute or two, Sam's crowd throughout the room was worked into a full frenzy of spiritual fervor. A woman stood up, her eyes closed, her palms outstretched in front of her facing upward to the heavens. The woman next to her sat wide-eyed, looking from me to her. If ever there was a test for which of these Christian students were the moderate ones and which were the Kool-Aid drinkers, this was it.

I stopped the music, which seemed to break the spell.

The standing woman blinked her eyes, looked around, and sat down. The people humming along with the music and swaying to Sam's words stopped abruptly. I'll never forget the look of absolute anger and resentment some flashed me when I shoved the CD back into Sam's coat pocket and told him to sit his ass down.

I thanked him for his contribution and told him never to do that ever again in my class. I said it all with a smile and patted Sam on the shoulder. He looked genuinely saddened at not being able to finish his sermon. I can only imagine the big finish he had planned.

He never showed up again.

He sent me emails from a mission trip he decided to embark upon at the end of the semester. In it he talked of health problems and being stuck in London for a bit, but he promised he would catch up when he got back. The day of the final came and went, and as I tabulated grades for the class, Sam had not a single grade to record.

Later that summer, his mother emailed me asking if Sam could make up the work. I pointed out that if it had simply been a test or two, I could possibly allow such a thing, but since Sam had only attended a handful of classes during the entire semester, had not turned in a single assignment, nor shown up for any of the exams, and decided to leave the country for three weeks at the end of the semester, there really wasn't anything to be done. Undeterred, she went to my department chair, demanding some scholastic form of Christian grace, and when he supported my position, she went to the dean. She and Sam argued that his illness prevented him from coming back from England. This would be one time where things did not go any further with a complaint to the dean, who did not ask me to do anything. It also happened to be the only time I knew of where a student tried to receive EVU's grace and failed. And no, I don't think that was a coincidence.

When White students brought their parents into the situation, I got summoned to the dean's office.

I had a student in my Introduction to Literature class who came to me early in the semester and told me his mom had cancer, and he had to take her to the doctor often. He said he would be missing some classes. I asked him how many classes, and he said he didn't know. My own mom had gone through breast cancer treatment, so I was sympathetic to his situation, but the red flag was that he didn't know what kind of cancer his own mom had. Figuring he was just a typically ignorant nineteen-year-old, I let that slide. I told him to let me know when he would be missing, and we could come up with plans to keep him up with readings and assignments. He never showed up or contacted me again until the last week of the semester.

I got a panicked email from the boy right before finals. I basically told him we couldn't do anything about the semester since he never came to class or turned in a single assignment, which were two papers, a midterm, and the upcoming final. Not to mention he hadn't heard about twelve weeks of my brilliantly enlightening lectures.

Obviously, he didn't show up to the final. But after finals week, I was notified by the dean's office that the student and his mother were complaining about me that I was being unfair during a difficult time for them. I was asked to extend "grace" to the student and let him turn in the missing work. So, reluctantly, I did.

A week later, I received his two papers. Each "paper" consisted of one short paragraph of three sentences, summarizing one of the texts. The paper topics asked students to take three of the readings and do various analyses about literary terms and cultural themes. So, a total of six sentences were turned in for the two papers. No sentence came close to addressing any of the paper topics. According to my detailed rubrics I used to grade those papers, he got zeros on both.

The midterm had two essay questions to be chosen from five topics. Each answer was to be about a page. He wrote two sentences. One for each essay question. One of the sentences was just a word salad which included the title of one of the stories and some random words.

The final had fewer sentences than the midterm.

After "grading" all the semester's work, I went to work crunching all those numbers and calculating the final grade to be a whopping zero for the semester. The F seemed generous, as "failure" implied some kind of attempt made.

A week later, I got a call from the dean's office. The mother, apparently a friend of the school, wanted to meet with me and the dean to justify my grading. Apparently, she was quite upset.

I went to the dean's office with the boy's work, along with examples of other student work from the semester. It seemed like overkill, but I knew what school I worked at. I knew that at an evangelical university that openly taught the prosperity gospel, I was the minority employee and the mom was the White paying customer.

The mom came in looking vibrant. I know not all cancer patients lose their hair, but she was fiery and seemed completely healthy. I told her I was sorry to hear about her cancer. She looked confused for a moment and looked over at her son. Then she looked back at me and said, "Oh, um, thank you."

She then lit into me saying she was once an English teacher who had personally educated her son, who she knew to be very bright. She accused me of having some kind of prejudice against her son and demanded to know exactly how I gave him an F for the semester. She looked over at the dean (who was an interim dean that semester) and made an accusatory remark about the hiring practices of the school, which was likely a feeble jab at my teaching qualifications or a veiled racist remark, or both—either way, she was making it personal. The interim dean smiled and said he was sure I had a rationale for the grade I gave. But that was all he would say for the meeting. I was on trial, and there would be no support from my administration that day. Not that I needed it in this case.

After the mom was finished, I pulled out the "work" her son had submitted. I showed her the "essays" he had written. I even read them out loud, which took about fifteen seconds. I showed her the essay prompts and pointed out the word count requirements, of which he was about 950 words short each, and the topics he was asked to consider. She took the single page of the essays from me and read them herself. After another fifteen seconds, she was done, but she must have sensed that reading two college essays should take longer, so she kept staring intently at the page for another fifteen seconds. Then she looked directly at me and said, "This is good work. I don't know how you can give this an F." After I put my eyes back into my head, I pulled out a few essays students had emailed me during the semester. I had crossed out the names, but I showed her how each one was approximately five

126

pages long. They had something called *thesis statements* and different paragraphs that cited the texts. They also happened to directly address the topics.

I shot a pleading look over to the interim dean, hoping he could give a ruling and dismiss us. He smiled and nodded for me to continue.

I showed the mom the midterm and final. A total of five sentences, none of which addressed the topics given. Just short, completely wrong, summaries of one short story each. I pointed out that one of the boy's answers didn't even come close to summarizing the story he had chosen to write about. He had clearly hoped I wouldn't read his sentence. Or maybe he had hoped that I, too, had not read the story before assigning it.

"This is good work," the mom repeated, though with a little less bravado.

I shot a now angry glance at the interim dean. He smiled and nodded.

I asked the mom, as an English teacher, if she could see the difference between the five-page essays that fulfilled the requirements of the assignment and her son's single paragraphs of three sentences. She started to crack, as I held the papers up next to her son's "work."

"Mmm . . . okay," she relented. "But don't you think an F is being a bit harsh?"

It took all my strength to not set the room on fire and to calmly tell her that, no, I did not think it was too harsh. After an awkward silence, the interim dean asked if anyone had any other questions. We filed out of his office in silence. I was proud of myself for not swearing, even once, during the meeting. I don't believe in God, but it's moments like this that force me to consider the possibility of his existence as I think about how no one, myself included, was injured and nothing was set ablaze that day. I was never able to bring myself to speak to that acting dean again. Amazingly, truth won the day, thanks to my ability to point out and make clear what would have been obvious to a five-year-old.

This is but one reason why I think there is a racial bias against Asian Americans at EVU. It's also why I was not surprised evangelicals universally voted for Donald Trump. Twice. They are masters at seeing value and worth where none exists.

## New Faculty, Same Old Shit

With my full-time position, I had to go through new-faculty orientation, even though I was perfectly familiar with the ins and outs of being a faculty member at the school. I had been fast-tracked through the system to be hired in the summer, which involved a meeting with the provost and president sitting with me for about forty-five minutes. They asked me about my church situation, and I told them we were attending All Saints. They laughed a little at that and mumbled something about honoring the liturgical style of church. When I told them I lived in Pasadena, they made jokes about me being wealthier than they were. I was a little confused because I was living in a lower-middle-class neighborhood in a 1,100 square-foot house. I would later learn the president was making $400,000 a year, and they were going to pay me $43,000 to be an assistant professor. Whatever. Neither of those men ever remembered meeting me over the next eight years, or if they did remember, they tended to just ignore me completely. I was so used to being invisible to White people, I wasn't even mad at that.

Despite treatment like that, I was happy and hopeful when I showed up to new-faculty orientation. It was a little bit awkward, because I had become the social person in the English department in the previous few years, helping with orienting and welcoming new faculty. I showed them around campus and around Pasadena. I even had new colleagues over to my house. And now some of those same colleagues were helping run the new-faculty orientation.

I can tell this story now that everyone involved has left EVU or been fired in a recent budget fiasco.

One of my colleagues, whom I befriended when she first came to EVU, had a house near the school that became what we called "the house of sin." The "sin" involved was just mild drinking and playing poker, but for EVU, it felt pretty darn taboo. Our group consisted of a few English profs, a guy from the School of Business, and a couple of dudes from theology/biblical studies. Don't get me wrong, they were all good Christians. They just held "liberal" views of drinking and gambling with small change.

After one of the new-faculty orientation meetings, my house of sin friend ran to where I was sitting and told me I just had to meet the new administrator. She said he was "one of us." His name was Craig Boyd, and he was from Saint Louis. He was to become the director of the Institute for Faith Integration, which was created to facilitate the integration of faith issues with academics, and he would go on to be both a member of our "sin" crew and a painful thorn in the side of the administration. Meeting Craig, who is still a close friend to this day, was the upside of the orientation week. The downside was being assigned another person who would be my faith integration mentor from the full-time faculty. I got a science prof who would eventually try to have me fired. Great guy.

## Two Roads Diverged in Southern California

As exciting as it was to be a new full-time faculty member at EVU with hopes for permanent employment in the English department, since the president and provost assured me they wanted me to be a permanent member of the faculty, my life outside of EVU was also entering a new phase. My kids were growing out of that toddler stage, potty training and becoming more independent, which gave Geri and me more freedom to do things like go out and take weekend trips.

I hadn't touched a guitar in many years, and I hadn't played regularly since my college days leading worship, so I was surprised when Geri got me a new interface to hook my guitar up to my computer. It basically made my computer into an amplifier. I dug out my old Stratocaster and fumbled around the frets, feeling a renewed elation from playing music again. I was horribly rusty, but it felt great.

I don't know if I believe in the concept of "manifesting" the things you really want to happen, but I started wondering how playing music could come back into my life. Being a regular at the Tuesday Night Café had reignited the fire to find creative outlets to correspond with and even drive my development as an Asian American devoted to social justice, equity, and inclusion.

And, in addition to all the interesting developments in my life, a proper rock star moved into the house across the street.

# 7

# Jesus Saves, But So Does Art

## UC San Diego, Price Center, 1990–1991 School Year

I got in line at the coffee shop in the Price Center, the brand-new student center. I didn't even like coffee that much, but I was starting to get used to it. These afternoon classes after lunch were tough, and Professor Sherley Anne Williams had ordered us all to get coffee before class when she noticed we were all looking like zombies. It was an African American literature class, and Professor Williams was herself a novelist and poet and a good friend of Alice Walker. I felt so fortunate to be in this class.

"I see you're taking my advice, Mr. Okamoto," I heard a voice behind me say. It was Professor Williams, of course. We chatted about coffee and general life stuff, and I couldn't believe I was just hanging with her. We walked to class with our coffees, and she started to ask about me and my life and background. I eventually told her I was a literature and writing major, and I was interested in taking her fiction writing class. She enthusiastically told me to sign up. But, she said with a knowing smile, she was tough on her writing students.

I would take three more classes with Professor Williams, and true to her word, she was tough. In literature classes, she wanted us to understand the Black experience and point of view as we read James Baldwin, Alice Walker, Toni Morrison, and Gloria Naylor. I learned so much about Black history and culture from Professor Williams, and I am grateful I got to know her even a little bit.

Around that same time, I was sitting in the food court of the Price Center with some friends when a tall man with dreadlocks, a long black coat, and sunglasses walked up to our table. My friends looked up at him, wide-eyed. It was my creative writing professor, Quincy Troupe, the American Book Award-winning writer and poet and recent "big name" hire in the English department.

"Yo, Scott. Walk with me. I have some ideas for your piece."

I gathered my things and walked with Quincy to his office, even though it was not his normal office hours. He checked his phone messages, and I distinctly heard a raspy voice say, "Call me back."

Now I was wide-eyed. "Was that . . . ?"

Quincy just nodded and took out some notes. He wanted to talk about my writing before he called Miles Davis back. I took three classes with Quincy, and he took an interest in my writing. There were very few BIPOC students in those classes, so I brought a unique perspective compared to most of my classmates. And Quincy brought his friends to class and to the school for events. I sat just a few feet away from Toni Morrison (I was too intimidated to say anything) and chatted with poet Paul Beatty. Quincy made sure to bring in writers of many races and ethnicities, so I also got to talk with Asian American writers David Mura and Garrett Hongo. Between his teaching of writing and bringing his amazing friends to class, I learned more about writing and the world than I ever thought possible.

And before we leave this flashback, I have to confess. I was also mentored by Dr. Lisa Lowe, the eminent Asian American scholar, and my goddamn Christianity fucked it up. Dr. Lowe believed in me and constantly encouraged me to write. Her Asian American literature class opened up a whole new lane in my mind, showing me the legacy of Asian American writers. And when she pointed me in the direction of focusing on Asian American identity, particularly in areas of sexuality and gender, I politely refused. It was not Christian to pursue such issues. There are many points in my past where I wish I could go back and smack the living shit out of my young, stupid Christian ass, and that one is in the top three.

# 2008: Dark Times For EVU

The political morale at EVU reached an all-time low leading up to the 2008 election because of Obama's strength at the polls. The mantra of the far-right side of the campus had gone from, "A vote for Bush is a vote for God," to, "Hey, no one's perfect." I occasionally heard people try to blame Bill Clinton for the sad state of the economy eight years after his presidency, but most students knew enough to know that George W. Bush had made huge mistakes. His approval ratings stayed in the low thirties for most of the end of his second term.

The Republican front-runner was John McCain, a moderate candidate from the right. He was known to champion immigrant rights and work with Democrats. But John McCain was not a Christian and never claimed to be. This was a dilemma for most evangelicals. Their mantra,

"A vote for Bush is a vote for God," could not be repackaged for the 2008 election. But this would be remedied for them in the most peculiar way.

Likely sensing the tepid support from Christians, McCain made a move that would change politics and the world forever. He picked Sarah Palin as his running mate. Before we all groan and clutch our heads at the memory, I do want to point something out. My wife and I were driving home from a fishing trip with the family, listening to satellite radio when Palin made her first address to the Republican National Convention. She praised women who had come before her, including Hillary Clinton. She sounded . . . rational.

Of course, she hasn't come within an Alaska mile of rationality since that moment. I always wondered what happened. In any case, evangelicals saw Palin's arrival as a direct sign from God. John McCain it was.

My own students mirrored the chaos of the rest of the nation's evangelicals. McCain wasn't a Christian, but Palin was. But Palin was a woman. Conservative Christians believe that women should not lead men, and if they won, Palin would be second in command over 150 million men.

But Obama.

Just his name caused severe anxiety in my conservative students. When students had to say it, they emphasized the second syllable, as if to point out the inherent evil in such a name. "O-BA-ma!" "O-BAAAA-ma!" "O-BAAAA-ma???"

I had a colleague in the Department of History and Sociology who seemed to be one of the most intelligent people at the school. She had a couple of different degrees, including a law degree, and she had come to evangelical Christianity only recently. As is usually the case when people come to Christianity later in life, her conversion must have been pretty intense. Like, a shade below the conversion of the apostle Paul. I say "seemed to be intelligent" because this otherwise intelligent person thought Sarah Palin was the most intelligent visionary ever in politics, so, like Paul, she was blinded during her conversion.

My sociology colleague asked me to be part of a panel discussion on politics leading up to the election. While chatting before the event, we talked about our kids. I mentioned how it was great that my kids, then eight and six, would see a Black man and a woman, Hillary Clinton, run for president. She stopped me and reminded me that Sarah Palin was also in the mix, as if Palin was more than just a running mate. I thought she was being sarcastic, so I laughed. And then I froze, feeling a jolt of horror as I studied her face. She was dead serious. As I've said, evangelical faith is a hell of a drug.

Similarly, a fellow woman adjunct in the English department was known to be a feminist. She claimed to be, anyway. But she overheard me lament one of the countless bizarre things Sarah Palin had said and got really angry at me. She pulled me aside in a hallway and lectured me about how unfair people were being to Palin.

Obama won decisively, and the next day was one of the most entertaining days I can remember at EVU. While whooping and cheers dominated the campus in 2004, the campus felt like a funeral in 2008. Students slumped up and down the Mascot Walk. They came to class and hugged each other for support. Some actually cried. "I hope he dies!" one girl shouted before class. "I hate him so much!" yelled someone else. "It's end times," a boy said as he sat down. "I hope you're all reading Revelations," said another, holding up his Bible as he came in.

Of course pretty much every minority was feeling what all the nice people, including John McCain, were feeling: inspiration and awe at the fact that a Black man was elected president of the United States of America. We traded smiles and discreet hugs. Other students in the Multi-Ethnic Programs celebrated by themselves in the office. A group of them were asked to leave an election watching event the night before because they were cheering. This was a small group of Black students in a room with hundreds of White students, and they were asked to leave because they were being "disrespectful." Never mind the campuswide celebrations in 2004. Cheering for Barack Hussein Obama making history would not be tolerated. Were any of the White conservatives encouraged, at all, about the giant leap for BIPOC people in America? No. No, they were not. Like, not at all. They were terrified. I guess I can't blame them. Their world was dramatically altered. It must have been terrifying to think of a Black family in the White House. Yeah. Fuck them.

Texting was becoming popular in 2008, and my freshmen students came to class all looking at their flip phones. Most were laughing. I noticed these moments of mirth in contrast with their otherwise dour faces and asked what they were laughing at. Some averted their eyes. The precious, clueless ones showed me their phones. The text message read, "Be sure to get your Obama Christmas ornaments today, so you can hang that ni**er from a tree."

I looked at the rest of the class and asked how many of them had received this text message. All but a few raised their hands. I asked my classes throughout the day, and most of the White students, and even many of the BIPOC students received this text. And most of them thought it was a funny, healing text that made them feel a little better after the country had handed the presidency to a satanic, Muslim, Nazi baby killer.

Despite that god-awful text going around, the frowns, tears, and malaise of the conservative White students sustained me for weeks. I walked around campus muttering under my breath, "Fuck you. You there, praying by the coffee shop . . . Fuck you. And you. You with the McCain/Palin 2008 sticker . . . yeah, fuck you. Fuck off to you, sir. And you." And if you're reading this and voted for McCain . . . fffffgood day to you.

It's not about John McCain, although fuck him for caving to the right-wing crazies and changing his mind about the Dream Act, which he, himself, helped create. It's that the politics of evangelical Christians had clearly taken on a new edge and suddenly become a real threat to the safety and well-being of people I cared about deeply.

My inner circle in the Tuesday Night Café was growing steadily through these years, and they were largely BIPOC and LGBTQIA. The rhetoric of Fox News and megachurch celebrity pastors was becoming more and more violent toward us. It wasn't just about "tax and spend" versus "fiscal responsibility" in politics anymore. It had become "us against them," something established by conservatives after Bush had said as much in a speech; and while he didn't mean exactly that, his followers and everyone in the GOP ran with that notion. They were somehow the keepers of American values, and being against them was to be against their White America.

## Evangelicals Slam the Door on My Way Out

Despite my reputation for being one of the Marxist liberals at EVU, I always tried to create classroom environments that were inclusive to everyone, including conservatives. Certainly, there have been students I just could not connect with. And of course, after the 2008 election, I had an entire section that made me consider driving off freeway overpasses on the way home each day.

During one semester, in the same section of freshman writing, I had a couple of students with bizarre views that defied all manner of logic and sense, and they made sure to express every facet of these views in the crudest terms. If you've ever taught a class, you know that each class takes on a vibe of its own. The personality of an overall class can be boisterous and fun with the right mix of students. Or it can be painfully quiet if most don't like to talk. Both scenarios bring with them challenges for a teacher to create a community of learning. And then there are sections of Freshman Writing where each student tries to outdo the others in levels of psychosis and calamity. That was this section.

The first student, we'll call her Sue, scared me the most. Since 2004, I had taken to trying to scare off any crazy conservatives on the first day of class. Given my run-ins with so many of them in the Fox News era, I just didn't want any students who would be unwilling to learn. So, on the first day of class, I would tell everyone that if there were any students who loved Fox News and were unwilling to hear some hard truths, they should leave, either at that moment or later that day. In the eleven years I did this, a few dozen students snatched up their belongings and stomped out of the room. After 2008, I switched to the Obama test. I would announce that if anyone truly believed Obama was the antichrist or a socialist dictator, or Hitler, and was unwilling to hear opposing views to these ideas, they should leave.

I honestly believe each of those students who fled those first days of class represent months of my life saved. Their angry, righteously indignant glares, I imagine, are the same looks the devil would get should he happen to encounter them. One year, a student dropped later that day, but her roommate stayed in the class. The next class session, the girl told me her roommate dropped because she thought I was pure evil. Her roommate had even called her parents to complain about me. I asked her if she herself was sure she was okay being in the class. She smiled and said she was.

Back to Sue. Sue had the same violent reaction to my introductory speech but decided it was up to her to save me. From myself. Instead of heading straight home to use her computer to drop the class, she wrote a seven-page email that is one of the saddest emails I've ever received from a student. In a patient and matronly tone, Sue explained to me how I had been badly deceived by the evil forces of this world. I noted that she didn't feel I warranted deception from Satan, himself. I had been duped, like a lot of well-meaning people, into overlooking the fact that our president, Barack Obama, was in fact, Hitler. She even attached a "research" paper she had written for her high school English class at a conservative Christian school, that proved that Obama's views were indisputably aligned with those of not only Hitler, but also Stalin, Mussolini, and Lenin. And Satan, of course. It almost went without saying.

Any political scientists and historians reading this are laughing out loud right now, as it is impossible to be incarnations of all those chaps all at once. Although Sue promised that over the course of the semester she would enlighten me to my ignorance, I never addressed the issue in class. I went around it and sniped at it. By the end of the semester, Sue seemed to be a changed person. But it was not as much me as the rest of the class that changed her.

Unfortunately, or fortunately, for Sue, she was in a section with a good mix of conservative proto-QAnons and BIPOC students that called her out on everything she said. There were times I didn't even have to say anything. On many days, Sue got pushback from the crazies who either misunderstood what she was saying or felt she was saying something liberal, and also from the BIPOC students who had grown accustomed to pointing out her dog-whistle-infused language regarding race.

The other precious student was a male student we'll call John. He was quiet and respectful to me, but he was prone to raise his hand and say the most bizarre things I had ever heard. As you might deduce at this point, that is saying quite a lot.

As if trying to outdo the "all Mexicans are lazy" dude from six years ago, John once said out loud, "The Native Americans were more than adequately compensated when we gave them reservations."

Yep.

If one had even the dullest imagination, he or she might imagine just how colorful the discussion could be in this particular class. Sue might say, "Those negroes (referring to Black people)," only to be cut off by the Latina students. "Did you just say 'negroes?'" John would roll his eyes at Sue's statements and then offer up a, "Women just need to shut up and . . ." only to be cut off, himself, by just about everyone else. My favorite outburst from him came when we were discussing the use of Native American identities as mascots for sports teams and schools. While discussing some articles criticizing the usage, John couldn't take it anymore. He gave a huge sigh and threw his hands in the air, as if he just couldn't take any more. I acknowledged him with a nervous smile.

"What about the Red Sox?" he said with the passion of a lawyer in a courtroom drama.

"What about them?" I asked, looking out at an equally puzzled class.

John looked at us all as if we were crazy.

"You don't have a problem with Red Sox or White Sox, right?"

I said I did not, and John launched into a minor tirade accusing me of being a hypocrite. I stopped him and asked what in the hell he was talking about. Was he actually comparing Native American human beings with . . . socks?

He was, indeed, and he pointed out that naming a team after socks was the same thing, so . . . and here he started to lose steam as his brain caught up with his ass and he realized there might be some fundamental differences between human people groups and socks. But it took a minute. Still, he halfheartedly continued arguing his case for the rest of the class time, which mercifully came to an end after a few minutes.

Add to this deranged duo a contingent of classic conservative evangelicals, and this was easily the most stressful class I had ever taught at EVU.

One innocent chap, while we were discussing issues of sex, said he could never marry a woman who was not a virgin. That was disturbing enough, but he had to go further, saying he didn't want to marry a "skank," eliciting another round of shouting and ranting.

I had a literature class right after this Freshman Writing Seminar class, and I would often open my book to find my hands still shaking from the verbal chaos I had just walked out of.

Of course, I would not be sharing this story if there hadn't been some kind of satisfactory resolution. Sue, despite her pledge at the beginning of the semester, evolved from an outspoken and sincerely crazy Glenn Beck parrot, to a broken, sullen outcast, to a thoughtful, if humble, participant in discussions at the end of the semester. In the middle, I was honestly worried about her, as it seemed her whole worldview was being dismantled by both my teaching and the class. I would walk past her on campus, and she would frown and look away or just offer a half-hearted greeting. I wrote her a few notes on her papers that encouraged her development of thought and praised her style of writing and willingness to grow in perspective. I saw her during finals week on the Mascot Walk, and she smiled warmly and wished me a Merry Christmas.

As for John, despite being slammed by me and the class repeatedly, he took my literature class the next semester. He was always eager to talk after class. When he had remarked about the plush accommodations we had given to Native Americans, I had assumed he was a racist of the worst sort. It turned out, he was speaking his ignorance, but was more than willing to be corrected and to learn. He had been to military school, so my sarcastic and professorial corrections were nothing compared to the discipline he had experienced there.

In both cases, I could perhaps talk about how my teaching helped these two individuals develop as thinkers and scholars. It would be tempting to launch into the details of my brilliant pedagogy and execution of outcome- and objective-based curriculum. It would also be misguided.

The point about the students and their ability to change is equally true about my own misconceptions about people. I had been burned so many times by zealous students bent on correcting their evil professor, I sometimes forgot that these were young, developing minds. To be sure, many of them were lost causes with no hope of ever thinking for themselves or escaping their ultraconservative views, be they political, theological, or both. But no matter how intellectually atrocious the views and thoughts expressed, there seemed to be no way of predicting where a given student would be at the end of a semester. When I got Sue's initial email, I was certain I had a crazy student who would cause me nothing but grief and strife. Certainly she caused a great deal of grief and strife, but watching her begin to see other points of view as valid was something I have come to understand to be the greatest reward at my job. She is still prone to her conservative views, I am sure, but at least she has been given, and has taken, the chance to expand her thinking. John uttered some of the vilest, most racist sentences I've ever heard in a classroom, and yet he took reprimands, rants, and accusations of racism and learned from them. Not only did he learn, but he also sought me out beyond the classroom to ask questions and talk about life.

If I had just yelled at him and called him names, I'm sure he could have gone further into his innocently racist views. But, as with Sue and all my students, I truly believe there is room to disagree, but we can still care about each other and listen. In some cases, we can even be friends. It was rare, but . . . yeah. It was really rare.

## SOMETHING HAPPENING HERE

I was already long done with evangelical Christianity by 2008, but the election shifted something in me. Whereas earlier I had been inclined to think most Christians were decent people who sometimes just needed a nudge or a metaphorical smack upside the head to become thoughtful, caring humans, I had now pretty much given up on the evangelical world altogether. I had come to better appreciate just how much these were mostly bad people with ill will toward the world outside their churches and outside of EVU. They were a driving political and social force for evil, and they needed to be stopped.

I redoubled my mission to fight this evil force by using Jesus against them. I pushed back against their bigotry. Not with my liberal ideology, no. The teachings and examples of Jesus were all I needed to shred their evangelical hatred of the world. If these kids came to EVU hoping to have their bigotry grown and reflected by their professors, and they did, I was going to throw the wrench into their plans and make them consider another way to approach their faith, simply by pointing out the inconsistencies in their own belief system.

And I had help.

Many students were seeing the same shit I was seeing and deciding to fight against it. The Multi-Ethnic Programs (MEP) were getting unexpected new life as BIPOC students came forward to lead the way in social justice and race issues. After Joy Hoffman left in 2006 to work at schools that didn't harm their students with policies and religion, EVU hired Joe Snell to be the director of MEP. Joe would become one of my closest friends at EVU and an invaluable supporter of students suffering at EVU.

Joe showed up at an APASO meeting one night and introduced himself to the ten or twelve of us there. I was impressed that a Black man was so enthusiastic about our little group and so well-versed in Asian and Asian American issues. In Joe's tiny office, I found a haven from the shit I dealt with every day at EVU, and I wasn't the only one. Joe listened to us and even shared our anger. I would go to his office and slump down in a chair, and Joe would nod, stop whatever he was doing, and listen. And when he put on programs to educate the campus on race issues, he would get vitriolic emails and voice messages from students and faculty, telling him he was doing Satan's work dividing the campus and succumbing to evil liberal causes. We listened to each other. At the end of our vent sessions, we often said we should get together for beers.

And one night, Joe came to my house, met my wife and kids, and we each drank two whole beers while we laughed and cried. This was significant because staff were not supposed to drink, and we were both lightweights. During a pause in our laughter, we overheard music coming from the other room where my kids were watching a Disney movie. Commercial-sounding gospel music blasted from the TV and we both winced.

"Man, why do White people always have to do gospel music?" Joe said gesturing toward the other room. He went on to complain about how it felt like EVU was co-opting his culture to seem cool.

Joe's big project was something he named UNLEARN Week, where the emphasis was on deconstructing the biases and assumptions we all have about race and identity. I thought it was genius because we weren't saying, "White people are racist." We were saying we all have perspectives to unpack, so let's unpack them together. Naturally, White people owned the lion's share of atrocities committed because of their abuse of their power, but hey. That's reality.

In 2008, when UNLEARN Week happened at the end of Joe's second year, it was a huge success, with hundreds of students attending the events put on by the multi-ethnic student organizations. APASO put on its first campuswide event, a panel of Asian American actors discussing the state of Asian American representation in the media. While I'd love to claim that my reputation as a popular professor brought out two-hundred-plus people to fill the large lecture hall, the reality is, the panel consisted of my friends, the writer, actor, activist traci kato-kiriyama, actor Junko Goda, poet and actor Edren Sumagaysay, musician Shin Kawasaki, and his awesome wife, actor Keiko Agena, whose *Gilmore Girls* fame was peaking at the time. Non-Asian students, faculty, staff, administration, so many people came to that event, mostly to see and meet Keiko, but far from it being a celebrity-worship event, everyone heard a sharp, unapologetic analysis of the state of Asian American representation in the media. And in 2008, such representation was pretty nonexistent.

More importantly, this event would mark the first of many times I brought my friends to EVU for an APASO event. As I look back on those days and years after that first event, I am so grateful to my friends for supporting me and the students at EVU, giving their time and their talents to students, most of whom could hardly appreciate what they were presenting. Evangelicalism is not only a hell of a drug; it's also a blinder that only allows its adherents to see fragments of the real world. None of the friends I brought to EVU identified as Christian, much less evangelical. But their worldviews, to my thinking, could only help to expand my students' love and care for the outside world they could neither see nor understand.

# ROCK 'N' ROLL MOVED ACROSS THE STREET

My world was expanding rapidly during this time. I was meeting more new faculty and bonding with them over the ridiculous evangelical culture we worked in, the MEP organizations were growing in both size and influence on campus, and my Tuesday Night Café community was growing up around me after several years of me being just around. I was now considered an "elder" in the community. traci would even come hang with me when I was on campus, and we would spend time writing, talking, and just watching the evangelical kids around us. Having her there and seeing EVU through her curious and artful eyes made me see just how ridiculous it all was. Whereas I knew and understood very well the homophobia, sexism, and racism of evangelical culture, traci, along with all my TNC friends, made me see how ugly, dangerous, and evil it all was.

So it just made sense when the abandoned house across the street from my own got fixed up and flipped, and a young twenty-six-year-old man moved in. We watched through our front window as his parents helped him carry furniture and boxes up the steps to his porch. He had scraggly hair and an ushanka cap that was popular with musicians. After a day or two, I brought a plate of cookies over to him, accompanied by my two then-toddlers, Ethan and Audrey. We welcomed him to the neighborhood and chatted a bit. I asked him what he did for a living, a loaded question because the housing market was reaching a peak, and the little house had to have cost a fortune at the time. He said he was a musician. He certainly looked the part. The thing is, in LA it seems like everyone is either a musician, an actor, a "producer," or the like. I figured I'd humor him, and I asked if his band played shows in the area. The Roxy? Coconut Teaser? He nodded and said they had played those places before and that they had just gotten off tour with Green Day.

I froze at that. Green Day? Like *the* Green Day?

After our chat, I ran back across the street with the kids and I googled him. Tim Pagnotta, singer of Sugarcult. Millions of records sold. There were videos, magazine interviews, and I knew some of his songs.

I asked my students if they had heard of Sugarcult. "Duh," was the response I got. They had headlined the Warped Tour, the biggest alt-rock tour at the time. The middle- and upper-class kids at EVU were part of the Sugarcult demographic. Well, the ones who were allowed to listen to secular music were, anyway. I had just gotten a major boost of cred because of my new neighbor.

Over time, Tim would become a member of our family. He invited me to some shows, and I got to know his bandmates. Geri and I became a sort of neighbor entourage, often hanging with the guys backstage and in their green rooms. I once walked with the band down a staircase that looked out at the venue and saw hundreds of fans screaming as we appeared. I wanted to shrink or disappear, not wanting to appear to be in the band, but I was also mesmerized. Seeing the adoring fans and later hearing them sing along to every song with such love was inspiring. The guys were used to it, but they appreciated it too. To me, creating something that meant so much to so many was both an honor and an accomplishment to be proud of.

Tim, and really all the guys—Marko, Airin, and Kenny—knew how to play the rock-star role, but they also knew how to separate their personal lives from their professional lives. While waiting to go onstage, they would engage me in deep conversations about politics and religion. They wanted to know all about life at EVU and how the Bush years had blended politics and evangelical Christianity, maybe forever. Marko was extremely well-read and a great writer himself; he kept the band's blog going, and he loved to talk about everything. Before one show, our conversation got really intense as we talked about how depressing the Iraq War was. I could hear the fans screaming when the door opened and a guy poked his head in and said, "Five minutes guys." I looked at Tim and Marko, who were deep in thought, and I asked if they wanted to stop talking so they could get into rock-star mode. They brushed that notion aside and kept talking. And when the door opened for them to hit the stage, Marko said, "We'll continue this discussion after we're done." They got up, grabbed their instruments, and went out and rocked as hard as they always did. I watched, in awe, from the side of the stage as they jumped, pranced, and played to the screaming, adoring fans. After the encore, I followed them back to the dressing room. We weren't even back in the room before Marko restarted our conversation. The ninety-minute intermission to our discussion hadn't broken his train of thought.

Tim was the perfect neighbor despite being quite a disappointing rock star. I would take breaks from grading papers to sit on his porch and talk about life. In the four years we lived across the street from him, he didn't throw a single party, much less a wild party, outside of his small wedding reception. Our shared love of home improvement and woodworking gave us plenty of time to talk over projects we helped each other with. I had found a third community. EVU, TNC, and Sugarcult.

It really felt like my life was building toward something as I grew my career at EVU and felt my community outside of EVU growing around me. I had found a beautiful balance between work, family, and community. And then in 2006, my wife shoved a little white stick into my face. I had had a vasectomy in 2004, and I had written a poem about it that ended up causing a bit of a stir at an English department event. Turns out there are two kinds of Christians: ones who find humor in poems about recovering from a vasectomy and ones who take great offense at poems about recovering from a vasectomy. I would not recommend referring to testicles ever in evangelical spaces, just to be safe. So it turns out a few swimmers evaded the cut vas deferens, the cauterized ends, and statistical improbabilities assigned to such a journey to the waiting egg in Geri's uterus.

If you're wondering how this happened, a vasectomy is supposed to be around 98 percent effective at preventing pregnancy. I am a 2-percenter. I got checked at six months, twelve months, and eighteen months, but I didn't make the two-year appointment. If you find yourself judging me for that, I have two things to say: (1) The regular sperm count test would not have revealed the very few swimmers in the mix. They needed a special test for that. (2) You try jerking off into a tiny plastic cup while two toddlers bang on your door asking for a snack.

So, we were having a third kid. Owen would be the best baby we had. He slept regularly and ate well, unlike Ethan and Audrey. But as great as life was with a new baby, excited two- and four-year-olds, a full-time teaching job and a vibrant community forming, the balanced life got tipped like a full canoe. Something had to go. Spoiler: it wasn't the baby.

EVU's days as a place for me were numbered, except for one rather epic last stand.

## THE MULTI-ETHNIC REVOLUTION BEGINS

When I first came to EVU in 1998, the campus seemed to me like a serene, eighty-eight percent White, cheerful, Christian place. Despite the universally held beliefs that homosexuality was a grave sin, liberals were likely deceived by Satan, and women were to be subservient to men, students were friendly to people—even Japanese Americans who

JESUS SAVES, BUT SO DOES ART

looked lost. A decade later, the evangelical culture had shifted from a welcoming, friendly vibe to an angry, fearful one, and much of that shift was due to the naturally convenient marriage between evangelicals and Fox News.

The lonely experiences of new students and visitors even caught the attention of the students at the school newspaper, the *EVU Tribune*, which decided to dabble in some investigative journalism to shine a light on the campus culture. And like the good Christian kids they were, they turned the issue into a good ol' Christian guilt story. There is a somewhat disingenuous narrative in Christian culture that says we should be better at recognizing the "least of these" as told in one of Jesus' lessons. It's a common theme in sermons, lessons, and testimonies, that we get too consumed with our own lives and fail to see a suffering brother or sister right in front of us. These days evangelicals spend way more time justifying their disdain for people suffering.

The *EVU Tribune* sent in an undercover reporter disguised as a punk rocker dude to walk the campus and meet with the admissions office to inquire about attending EVU. They outfitted the male student with a fake mohawk, fake tattoos, and fake piercings, and because evangelicals tend to know very little about the world outside of their church circles, the good kids on the *EVU Tribune* editorial staff made this punk rocker . . . gay. Yes, in order to make sure they covered all of the socially undesirable identities for an evangelical university, they covered their bets with everything they could think of. The fact that punk rockers historically tend toward the homophobic end of the social spectrum eluded them. It wasn't clear that there were any physical markings indicating his sexuality, so one can only assume that the kid made a point of telling everyone he encountered that he was gay.

So, the undercover school newspaper operative suited up and hit the cafeteria first. He paid for a lunch and looked for a seat. The article noted dramatically that no one offered him a seat, much less welcomed him to the school. He stood out enough that a few of the good

Samaritan Christian types approached him to talk to him. The same might have happened if a homeless person entered the cafeteria. In an evangelical setting, there is always someone looking to pad their testimony with an opportunity to talk to "the least of these" in society. Overall, the article noted the isolation the kid felt walking the campus and eating a meal. Never mind that punk rockers are often antisocial or that most rational human beings might not want to sit next to one.

The grand finale was heading over to the admissions office to see about attending the school. I'm sure the admissions folks wondered why in God's good name this boy would ever want to attend a school like EVU. But they were polite, if confused, when they talked to him about their Christianity. At some point, he identified himself as, in addition to being gay, atheist. The *EVU Tribune* staff was taking no chances to get a story out of this. In the end, the kid walked off campus—beneath the careful watch of Campus Security, I'm sure—and into the pages of a heartfelt plea for EVU students to be more welcoming.

I tell this story to make a number of points, mostly about race, even though the lack of cultural intelligence and the contrived journalism could spring to the forefront of any analysis of the story. In general, the gay punk-rock atheist kid was treated the same way any solo person would be treated walking cold into a campus cafeteria and unannounced into an admissions office. In fact, he was given a lot more attention than a "normal" person doing the same thing. It would be a lonely endeavor for anyone to try this. Try walking into any college cafeteria and see how you fare. But if they had added race into the mix, they would have had a much more enlightening and relevant story. Many BIPOC students at EVU live each day feeling isolated and unwelcomed. When they are engaged they endure stupid questions about their backgrounds. Black students always—and I mean always—got asked if they were at the school on scholarship or for athletics. Asian American students often felt invisible. At least the punk-rock atheist homosexual got attention. I'm going to assume Asian American students would not want to dress up as punk rockers to get more attention. Still, the fact that the White reporters for the *EVU Tribune* felt the need to invent a whole new kind of human being when they could have just used a BIPOC person to get the same or even a better story tells you everything you need to know about the culture. It tells you more than the actual article, and it tells you there were likely no BIPOC people on the *EVU Tribune* staff at that time.

Ethnic organizations, up to that point, were mainly quiet refuges from the White noise of campus. If there was any discussion of the overt racism of the campus culture, it was in hushed silence, even in the school paper. It had been important to curate ethnic spaces because of the overwhelming White culture that would not tolerate any pushback to its supremacy. So, when White professors said racist things, a horrifyingly common occurrence, there was no school response.

When a Pakistani student complained that his professor was calling him Apu, after the controversial *Simpsons* character, the department did nothing. And when the student went to the dean, the professor was told not to call him that because the student was "sensitive." When a White history professor spoke lovingly of the "Go west, young man" notion of manifest destiny because it brought "light" to "dark" places, the one woman who complained got made fun of—by the professor.

And when students in the dorms shouted "ching chong" at Asian American students, nothing happened, except for the Asian American students smiling sheepishly. When White boys decided they could use the N-word because they were friends with a Black student in their hall, nothing happened. When Latino students were called "beaners" or "illegals," nothing happened. Nothing ever fucking (adverb) happened.

And after the 2008 election and the racist events that followed, some students had had enough. The school held a town-hall meeting, led by the beloved university president, in which he addressed issues of racism on campus. In the weeks after the election, I was hearing reports of harassment and name-calling from the BIPOC students, and a couple of different stories involving swastikas. In one, Black and other students of color reported having swastikas drawn on their cars in the EVU parking lot. In another, a student of mine rode to school in a car that had a Confederate flag with a swastika inside it painted on the rear windshield. It was his roommate's car, and even though students reported the car every day for a week, the school did nothing about it. It took an article in the *EVU Tribune*, which was finally paying attention, detailing all these incidents to get the administration to act.

At the town-hall meeting, the school president sat before hundreds of students and listened as, one by one, they came forward and told their stories of racism and abuse from faculty and classmates. He seemed saddened and shocked to hear this, and he promised to do something. Despite the fact that he was not the person to be complaining to, or the person who could actually do anything, the students took solace in the idea that the school was finally listening to them. What they didn't know was that the president was both unwilling to do anything and not in a position to make sweeping changes apart from the board of trustees.

One notable voice from the night was president of AMIGOS (A Mixed Intercultural Group Of Students), which was a conservative ethnic organization that held salsa dancing and worship nights in Spanish. The president cried as she talked about feeling completely unsupported by the school as she dealt with overt racism from classmates and professors.

A student named Matthew Gonzalez was at the town hall, and he was moved to join AMIGOS to help. But with the group's president graduating, Matt took the opportunity to recruit his roommates, Rod Olmeda Lopez and Jonathan Garcia, to retool and rename AMIGOS into LASA, the Latin American Student Association. LASA would change the cultural landscape of EVU for many years.

At the same time, another student named Abbie Cirelli was rapidly deconstructing her faith. She had gone from a passionate evangelical who was homeschooled to a feminist and queer advocate in just a couple of years. She started writing for the *EVU Tribune*, shedding light on issues of identity, and she joined forces with Matt and a few others to start an underground org, then named Gay/Straight Alliance. The GSA would serve as a secret group to support the many struggling students who were coming to terms with their identities.

My APASO gang was coming around too. Led by Sammie Howell, a part-Filipina woman, Ryan Chin, and many others, the group would join forces with the multi-ethnic organizations to fight against the new, angry, openly bigoted conservative culture at EVU. We had a faculty leader in Joe Snell, we had the student leaders in place, and we had a climate that seemed to be begging for a righteous smackdown.

What could possibly go wrong?

# God Gave Rock 'n' Roll Back to Me

Life outside of EVU got a lot more interesting around this time. My friend Shin Kawasaki, who had come to the first APASO event with his wife, Keiko Agena, started a weekly jam session at the Grandstar Jazz club in Chinatown. At first it was a bunch of DJs with a few musicians, but Shin transformed the scene into an evening of mostly freeform jams with musicians of all levels.

The universe seemed to be pushing me back to playing music with Tim moving across the street and now Shin encouraging me to bring my old Stratocaster and amp to his jam session, which he called Midtones. I started playing regularly and was thrilled to learn that I was getting a lot better at guitar just by playing with amazing musicians from Shin's world. These were musicians who could play a whole song, note for note, if they had heard it once before. Pop music was easy for them, so they often launched into jazz standards and classics. It was a friendly kind of scene where Shin could call someone up to sing any-thing from Led Zeppelin to Britney Spears and enough musicians in the room could play the song flawlessly for the singer in live karaoke.

Each semester, there would be one day every other week where I would sleepily drive to work to teach early-morning classes after hav-ing been at Midtones until 2:00 a.m. the night/morning before, my ears still ringing from the loud music. And it was always worth it. The rela-tionships formed during those years are some of the deepest I have ever experienced.

Through this space, which overlapped with the Tuesday Night Café, I met the friends who would form a side project at Midtones called B-Squad, comprised of us nonprofessional musicians. We would do eighties and nineties covers, often poorly, but damn was it fun. We would rehearse at our community rehearsal space and then get to per-form at Grandstar, usually at the end of a Midtones session. B-Squad would last a couple of years before it became Band Moto, a band where we wrote original songs. I still play music with those friends at the time of this writing.

With all the shit happening at EVU, the contrast to life outside balanced with a young family, rich creative endeavors, and amazing community, it felt like something would need to give. And it wasn't going to be my family, music, or community.

# 8

# A Brief Revolution

University of San Francisco, Master of Arts in Writing Class, 1996

It was my turn to read my work in a personal narrative class. I had written about a family trip to Hawaii we'd taken when I was around ten years old. We went on the Pearl Harbor tour, and while cruising through the harbor, the tour guide gave facts about each ship and how they fared during the attack that would launch the US into World War II. At some point, I noticed a group of White families glaring at our young Japanese American family. The hatred in their eyes hit me hard, as I realized they were looking at us as enemies of America, a country I loved deeply. I finished reading my piece about this trip, and looked up at my classmates. The first fellow student to give her feedback was unmoved at the content. She stared at the pages I had handed out, shuffling the papers as if she were looking for something.

"I'm just not hearing the 'Asian' in your voice," she began. "I was really looking forward to hearing that, and not hearing it was really disappointing."

I sat for a moment, not knowing how to respond. What the fuck was an "Asian" voice? I wanted to ask her what she meant, but I had this horrible feeling that I was supposed to know. I was not yet self-aware in my identity as an Asian American of Japanese descent, but fortunately, some White classmates had my back.

"What are you asking?" one friend in the class demanded. "Is he supposed to read in an accent?"

The critical woman shook her head. It wasn't that. She cited Amy Tan and her soft, poetic voice and how it reflected the "Asian" culture.

"Asian culture?" another classmate shot back. "What even is that?"

After a few minutes of grilling the woman, we moved on. I was left feeling confused. I had worked long and hard to develop a voice that was just me. Several classmates had chimed in saying they found the story to be moving and well-written, but I couldn't shake the ugly feeling that I was expected by some to be something I wasn't.

Of course, I would go on to learn that the assumptions people have about Asian American men play a crucial role in how we are treated and regarded. And, naturally, EVU would be the perfect place to reinforce it all. It would also be the foil I needed to figure it out.

# THE BEGINNING OF THE END FOR MULTI-ETHNIC PROGRAMS

A week before the 2009 school year, I got an EVU news alert on my phone. Joe Snell, the beloved director of the Multi-Ethnic Programs and my closest friend at EVU, had died of a heart condition while at a lunch meeting. He had had a defect in his heart his whole life, but he didn't tell many people about it, choosing to live his life to its fullest each day. I was at a swimming party with my kids when I read the message, and I just froze, staring at my phone for several minutes. My kids saw my tears and asked what was wrong, but I couldn't find my voice.

I immediately reached out to everyone I knew in MEP, just wanting to connect with those I knew felt the way I did. It was more than shock and grief from losing a friend. It was also the horrible feeling that BIPOC students at EVU would never recover from this loss. Joe's passing, sadly, did end up being the beginning of the end for the Multi-Ethnic Programs office.

Because this was EVU, there would be more pain in the aftermath of Joe's passing. The ethnic organizations began planning a memorial service for Joe, and the tone of the event reflected the anger and passion everyone felt, coupled with the tremendous feelings of sadness and loss for the school. Each ethnic organization planned to contribute a portion of the service. And then the school stepped in and assumed control. Joe's memorial service was now being planned and executed by Chapel Programs, the office that put on chapel services, with people who did not know him like we did. The anger of the students had been simmering as they planned the service, but it boiled over when the school took over. Many who had planned to share stories, songs, or poems refused to participate or simply didn't show up. Others forced their way onto the program.

Sammie Howell was the president of the Asian Pacific American Student Organization (APASO). She had come to EVU, like most students, as a fired up evangelical, but her experiences led her to quickly deconstruct her faith. When she discovered APASO, it was led by a solid team of Asian Americans and Black students who were passionate about the issues. As she said when she was a guest on my podcast, *Chapel Probation*, she had found her people. As a young woman of mixed race, she heavily identified with her Filipino side, and APASO was a place for her to explore that identity away from the maddening ignorance and microaggressions of White EVU culture.

Joe Snell would be an invaluable mentor to Sammie, helping her guide APASO with a focus on building coalitions with the other ethnic organizations. When Joe died, Sammie was one of the students hit hardest. It made perfect sense to have her speak at Joe's service.

On the day of Joe's memorial service, now an official EVU chapel service, the president of the school sat next to us and looked sad, even though he barely knew Joe. He gave a short, vague talk about how good a person Joe was. In an irony that only a few of us understood, the gospel choir showed up ready to dazzle with several songs prepared. I guess you can't ask a huge choir of several dozen students to come and just do one song. At one point, they launched into a loud, fast celebration song with soloists and dancing and clapping. They exhorted us all to stand and clap. Even though I was sitting next to the school president, I stayed in my seat. I would not participate with a choir that didn't know Joe, next to a president who didn't know Joe, in a service we didn't plan. And I really didn't feel like fucking (adverb) dancing in celebration at that moment. I looked around the auditorium and saw several others who remained seated, a look of pain and shock on their faces. In all, the gospel choir did three long songs throughout the night. A lot of us got up and paid tribute to Joe. Some expressed anger at the school. Some just expressed their sadness at losing the only person in Student Life who listened to them. I mumbled a tribute to my friend through tears and a shaky voice. The students actually hit EVU the hardest. Embedded in their tributes to everything Joe meant to them was the obvious implication that the school had lost one of its only staffers who had a working relationship with the BIPOC students.

Sammie went after the school hard. In front of the president and a few other administrators, she lit into the school, calling out the racism in the culture and the classrooms. She said Joe was one of the few people to listen to students like her. The common theme in all our tributes to Joe was that he was irreplaceable. This would be proven to be true in short order.

# The LASA Incident

Students Matthew Gonzalez, Rod Olmeda Lopez, and Jonathan Garcia had launched the Latin American Student Association that same year. With a renewed focus on identity and political engagement, they immediately transformed the group from a conservative evangelical social club into a force for change. For as long as I had been there, White evangelicals at EVU had always been, by and large, anti-Black and anti-Brown. Racism against both groups was common in my classes and in the living areas, and Matthew, Rod, and Jonathan were done taking it. They called out racism when they saw it. They collaborated with APASO and the Black Student Association (BSA) to promote events. And they went to work on the administration to alter the school policies to be more inclusive.

Shortly after Joe died, Rod had the idea of making a Día de los Muertos *ofrenda*, an ornate display, to honor Joe. To those who know what the holiday is, Día de los Muertos is simply a cultural day to honor those who have died. To evangelicals, the day is a pagan, even satanic, ritual. Rod erected a display with Joe's picture and some flowers and placed it on an outdoor stage near the center of the main campus. The school, led by the Student Life staff, called the LASA boys in to explain what the *ofrenda* was, exactly. Of course they didn't know, and of course they were suspicious of anything Brown. In truth, it was simply a picture with some flowers. But after the meeting, the staff and administration came to the conclusion that the *ofrenda* was part of a pagan ritual and had to be taken down.

And thus the war between LASA and EVU began. Everything was in place for the first time in the history of the school. It had started the year before when the school held the town-hall meeting in the wake of the swastika incidents. Students saw and heard other students decry the overt racism and all-around bigotry on campus, and they realized that they could find each other and band together to fight back. For the first time in the school's history, conservative White students felt uneasy.

With LASA now formed, BSA branched into several smaller groups with different emphases, and even the normally conservative kids in APASO got fired up. The Multi-Ethnic Programs kids had been galvanized, and when the Día de los Muertos incident happened, the school had no idea it had ignited a firestorm it could never have imagined in its worst nightmares. Before that point, there had never been students of color united to educate themselves and to share resources to fight systemic racism. The students of color at EVU had always taken the evangelical view that the best way to handle racism and oppression was just to love the school, but Matthew, Rod, and Jonathan had taken it upon themselves to read up on revolutionary figures in Latin American history. I even shared a textbook from my undergraduate days from when I took a Chicano literature course. They took on the culture of the school the way I had always wished APASO would. They were unapologetic and tough.

So, as soon as the school labeled the *ofrenda* pagan, it was on. The LASA kids dressed up in black with skeletons painted on their faces to go to chapel. An ally on the *EVU Tribune* staff, Abbie Cirelli, wrote up a full center-spread article about the issue. Each of the ethnic organizations supported LASA, and the LASA boys met with administrators to make their case.

And for the second year in a row, the school held a town-hall meeting to tamp down what was becoming a bigger and bigger issue on campus, and, unfortunately, it knew exactly what to do.

The president of the school, once again, sat on a stool in front of an angry auditorium and listened sympathetically as dozens of students raged. But this time he had help. A Latino board of trustees member and another administrator joined him. All they did was listen, nod, express sympathy, and ultimately shake their heads and just say, "No."

"Sorry, but no."

"We hear you, but no."

"You're making excellent points, but no."

*No. Fucking. Way.*

I'm paraphrasing, but that was essentially the message. *Fuck off.*

Matthew made the argument that many things allowed on campus had pagan roots but were no longer seen as pagan. Halloween-based events were absolutely allowed on campus, despite their pagan roots. Bonfires around which people sang worship songs could be traced to pagan rituals and human sacrifices. Even Christmas has pagan roots with its use of trees decorated with colorful ornaments and with gifts placed beneath them. But when the Latin American Student Association did the exact same thing, the school could not see that they were doing the same thing White folks do with pagan traditions. LASA was being punished for being Brown.

The worst part of the whole thing was the hope the students had that their voices, their organizing, and their point of view could make a difference. But the school used a wealthy, powerful, Mexican American board member who, of course, was against the Día de los Muertos tribute to Joe Snell. He was all too happy to side with his White masters and administer the final blow to the cause. If the one Mexican American board member was against it, there was nothing to do but take the display down and accept defeat.

I went to the meeting, and I walked out halfway through as I realized what was happening. Students were pouring their hearts out in good faith before the president and his people who sat there looking sympathetic, but it became clear right away that they were not there to change their position. They were there to enforce it. While many students said they felt heard, I saw through it. The school was pretending to do their due diligence while not even considering a change of heart. As the president was explaining for the seventh or eighth time the school's position, I got up, locked eyes with him, and walked out. I couldn't watch the students get gaslit any longer.

First the swastika meeting, and now this. The students eventually received the message loud and clear. Change was not going to happen under this administration and this board of trustees. And without Joe Snell, a staff member who believed in the cause, there would be no one to lead another revolution. This generation of students, for my money the greatest advocates for social justice ever at EVU, would graduate, and EVU would go back to business as usual. And MEP would die a quick death in the coming years.

# THE ANGRY ASIAN AWAKENS

Obviously, I no longer considered myself part of this Christian enterprise at this point, but I was only vaguely conscious of how I was growing and developing as a progressive-minded Asian American man. Every day, everything around me reinforced the notion that I was an outsider at best and a suspicious immigrant at worst. Finding my people in the Tuesday Night Café world had opened my eyes to the fact that I was never going to really belong in a place like EVU, and it wasn't because of anything I was doing. Evangelical culture was simply built to uphold White supremacy. At best, I could only hope to blend into the shadows, get a paycheck, and work from the fringes.

There was another option to gain credibility as a BIPOC influencer. Evangelical celebrities like Francis Chan pandered to the White gaze, making Asian jokes and arguing that racism didn't exist or didn't matter. There was no way I was doing that shit.

One semester, the English department sent me to talk to the head librarian at EVU to discuss the partnership between the library and the Freshman Writing Program. The library had been assigning a librarian to each section of the course to do a one-hour introduction to the library and basic research. It was a hit-and-miss endeavor, with some professors reporting they loved the program and others hating it. Students universally hated it. I was tasked by the English department with suggesting some new ideas and reviewing what was working for the English department and what was not. In particular, a significant portion of the one-hour class session was spent reading through some handouts from a dry, boring handbook the librarians had put together, which outlined the information they read to the students. Students were known to be restless during this portion. My students were often downright cranky. We wanted to explore what the course would be like without it.

At one point during my short meeting with the head librarian, she referred to her handbook in between us for the umpteenth time, and I put my hand on it and said, "Let's pretend this doesn't exist." I asked her to brainstorm with me based on the outcomes and objectives of the partnership in order to see what we could do differently to make them happen, and to engage the students. I was really hoping we could talk independently of the handbook. But she couldn't let it go. She just kept saying, "But in the handbook it says . . ." I gave up and went back to the department chair and the director of Freshman Writing to tell them I had failed at getting anything done. I don't even think the head librarian understood what I was trying to discuss. For her, the sun rose and set on her handbook. That shitty, boring handbook.

When I met with the director of Freshman Writing, he said the librarian had called him that day to report to him that I had been rude and out of control. We both had to laugh at that, since he knew me well. It seems that my polite, gentle demeanor had come off as threatening. Because I wasn't the non-confrontational, quiet Asian, I had become something dangerous and foreign. She did seem uncomfortable, I remember, and this made me be even more gentle and earnest in my desire to communicate what the department, not just me, wanted to accomplish with its partnership with the library. But because I did not bow or respectfully submit to her handbook authority, she saw me as a scary threat.

It seemed like I was two things at once. With other minorities, I was a nearly invisible and rather inconsequential entity. With ignorant White and non-Asian folks, I was just plain scary, particularly if I was in a place of authority—in this case, representing the Department of English.

Pedagogically, I resented White professors and the librarians who felt they could just read something to students and be respected as educators. As an Asian American man, I had to prepare engaging, often downright hilarious classes that were academically on point to be accepted as an educator. I knew what EVU expected in Asian Americans, and it wasn't much. The idea that a White librarian felt he or she could just come in and recite a bunch of policies and procedures grated on me. Often, students would turn in their seats and just glare at me during the library sessions, as if to say, "What the fuck is this?" Now, the students definitely had a generational and cultural expectation that they were paying customers who needed to be dazzled and entertained during their college experience, and I'm not defending that. But I was good at entertaining. At the very least, I prepared classes that entertained myself. And I didn't read out of a handbook.

As a full-time assistant professor, I flexed my humor and command of argumentation in Freshman Writing classes and my insights and love for literature in the other classes. Now, keenly aware of my Asian American identity for the first time in my life, I was on a mission to challenge the assumptions my students had about everything. Me, them, their faith, the Bible, American culture, everything.

I realized that my background prepared me for this moment. My UCSD classes with Quincy Troupe, Sherley Ann Williams, Lisa Lowe, and many others gave me a foundational understanding of race and ethnic identity. My new friends at the Tuesday Night Café gave me a setting to grow those concepts into more meaningful and deeper relationships and community. And EVU . . . stood in complete contrast to everything I wanted my life to be. It was getting more "diverse" with the percentage of White folks plummeting down to the high seventies level in population, from the eighty-eight percent when I first arrived. But goddamn, it still felt completely dominated by Whiteness—and those BIPOC faculty, staff, and students who would uphold Whiteness.

# THE FACULTY OF COLOR GROUP . . . KIND OF SUCKED

The 2008 election seemed to magnify the idea that *diversity* was a Black and White issue. White conservatives at the school felt justified in putting their anti-Blackness on full display, and Black faculty and staff felt emboldened to stand up for themselves. Lost in this battle were the rest of us. It was painfully clear that we did not matter.

It was around this time that the school put together something called the Faculty of Color Group. Started by the associate provost for diversity, it was supposed to be a resource for the BIPOC faculty. No White faculty were allowed unless they were presenting some kind of "leg up" for us sad, woeful, non-White faculty. I went, mostly out of an obligation to support one of the leaders, a Korean American woman I had gotten to know, but I didn't speak up much at first. In truth, I felt as invisible in those meetings as I did in the full-faculty meetings. I was the only Asian American man to participate in the group.

Although no White people were allowed to come to the meetings, they were present in our collective colonized minds. Anything that takes place at EVU takes place in a context dominated by Whiteness. It's either literally a White setting or it is in contrast to a White setting. Nothing happens outside of a White context. Not even a Faculty of Color Group.

Sitting in the middle of a conference room on South Campus at those meetings, there was a giddiness in the air, and it felt like we were getting away with something, or we were breaking some kind of rule. I would sit next to the smiling guy from Korea who kept asking me how I spoke English so well. He was blissfully oblivious to the irony that such questions usually come from ignorant White people. I told him I was born here and only White people ask that question. He laughed and said it must be a good question then. The group was mostly African and African American. In second place was the Latino faculty. Anyone who has experience with diversity issues in a Christian setting operates under the assumptions that Christians are usually a few decades behind the rest of the world in areas of diversity, and that diversity is a Black and White and sometimes Brown issue.

Despite being painfully aware of the many assumptions about my identity, I eventually spoke up more often at the Faculty of Color meetings. I even rigorously disagreed with my Black and Latino colleagues on matters of policy and various issues. The smiling professor from Korea approached me after one of the meetings. He was in awe of me, and he asked how I was able to speak with such force, even though I was, as he put it, "oriental." I shrugged and said, "I just had to teach myself."

I generally stayed invisible. One year, as a cochair of a national conference on diversity, a national conference put on by the Faculty of Color Group, I raised my hand and pointed out a potential problem with the way we were organizing some part of it. There was silence, as if what I said didn't quite register. No one responded to my observation, and the discussion moved on to other points. A few minutes later, another colleague, who was not Asian, made the exact same observation I had. Everyone nodded. People said, "Oh, that's a good point! I'm glad you caught that!" A Black professor whom I had gotten to know looked over at me quizzically from across the room and mouthed, "Didn't you just say that?" I shrugged.

At the national conference we held, where I was one of three chairs, the Black associate provost for diversity gave a concluding talk and handed out certificates of recognition to the other two chairs, thanking them for their hard work. Before she finished, several people shouted out, "What about Scott?" The associate provost just said, "Oh, yeah. And Scott," and ended the conference. I was invisible even when I was a cochair at a national conference with my name in the front of the program.

And then I quit the Faculty of Color Group at EVU. I still didn't like the fact that White people were not invited to attend, unless they were invited to speak. And the group never became the support that I thought it would be. It became a "let's get a leg up on the White folks" kind of group. Worse, it often felt like extra help to keep up with the White folks. I wasn't interested in having administrators come in and give advice on how to fill out our faculty evaluation sheets for maximum scores, or tell us how to apply for a Fulbright Scholarship.

If you know anything about higher education, you might be thinking that a lot of these problems with race happen at all schools, not just Christian ones like EVU. And you'd be correct. I taught for seven years at a local community college, and every semester I had to go to a basement office to either turn in or pick up a classroom key. The Asian American woman eventually started to remember me, but for the first three years I would show up at her window, and she would say, "Math department, right?" The first few times, I would tell her I was in the English department, and she would look confused and irritated for a moment before shrugging and giving me my key. The form I always filled out said I was in the English department, but in her mind, I had to be a math professor. Apparently, reading is not always believing. Each time she did this, she looked down at the key acquisition form and then looked at me like she was annoyed or disturbed. Like I had somehow messed up her neatly categorized world order in her mind. So, even our own people are not immune to the lazy White assumptions that exist about Asian Americans.

Christians schools are just as frustrating when it comes to race issues, but I found it to be a lot more infuriating because there is the claim that they are all God's people. Spend some time in a predominantly White Christian setting, and you will eventually conclude that God's people are White, but the rest of us can learn to act and sound like them. We can be honorary God's people, present but separate from the majority culture. In other words, to be evangelical in America is to give yourself to White supremacy.

With this realization that evangelical culture promotes White supremacy, my own sense of purpose to fight it and expose it grew stronger every day.

# The Sisters Nine

It would be fair to wonder what in the world was keeping me at this school for, at this point, ten years. Shitty colleagues, shitty students, White supremacist evangelical culture . . . what would keep a worldly, intelligent, caring human being in this setting? Well, let me tell you about the good kids. Or the "bad" kids, depending on who you ask. To me they were some of the best people I've ever met. In addition to being completely devoted to the Multi-Ethnic Programs students and the secretive LGBTQIA students, several groups of students existed outside of EVU's fundamentalist culture.

Lily introduced herself to me in the parking lot as I was getting out of my car. She was an English major and was one of those free spirits who people just fell in love with. She usually strode through the campus with an entourage of seven to ten young men behind her, but on this day, she was alone. I locked my car and suddenly heard an angelic voice. "Okamoto! Here's some poetry for you."

I turned to see Lily walking toward me, reciting something that sounded like Victorian poetry. We walked across the parking lot exchanging pleasantries, and I learned that she was introducing herself to all the English faculty. I had to admire this kid's enthusiasm, and I didn't have the heart to tell her I mainly taught the lower division courses. This chance meeting in the parking lot, though, would be my introduction into a group of students living outside of the EVU bubble, even as they went to class inside of it.

Later, when a colleague had to go on maternity leave, I was asked to teach her creative writing and Shakespeare classes, both of which I had never taught. The creative writing class was right up my alley, as I have a Master of Arts in writing from the University of San Francisco.

That first semester teaching creative writing was the single greatest teaching experience I've ever had. The students bonded with me and with each other in a way I had never experienced and never would again. I encouraged them to write whatever they wanted, running workshops as a class and in small groups. They impressed me with their stories of love, hate, sex, science fiction, so many different genres. I pushed them to expand their use of language and imagination. No limits. I'm still Facebook friends with about three-quarters of that class. But the person who became a close friend was a young woman with dyed black hair cut short with bangs. She sat in the back and made strange faces at everything I said, and I made it a personal mission to get her to laugh or smile.

Kristin approached me about reading more of her writing outside of class, and I was so flattered that she didn't hate me, that I agreed. She was Lily's closest friend, and I found myself getting coffee with the two of them and talking about life and writing.

Through Kristin and Lily, I met the rest of their community that formed out of a dissatisfaction with the ethos and course offerings of EVU's English department. They were the misfits who didn't subscribe to purity culture or evangelical fundamentalism, and they could write and think as well as anyone I've ever met. With the shackles of conservative Christianity removed, they pushed each other to write and create incredible poetry, prose, and music.

One of the people who reached out to me was Ella Baker, a then pre-trans student who would become a friend a decade before fully transitioning, and who would amaze me with her writing and life perspective. Ella approached me about doing an independent study in creative writing, so we met every week on the Mascot Walk and workshopped her writing. More importantly, we just talked about life and identity. Finding someone who saw evangelical Christianity as an insidious force for evil in the world and was willing to talk openly about it was a huge help to me. It helped to clarify my identity and my role as an English professor.

The group called themselves "the Sisters Nine," and they met regularly, bringing their writing to share, most of which was done outside of their classwork. They may have been the countercultural "sinners" who had abandoned most of their Christian faith, but they were wholly devoted to their craft.

I was often invited to join the Sisters Nine, first at an on-campus apartment and later at a yellow off-campus house. There I took hits of weed with them in a communal ritual of clearing the heads before we shared our writing. They even had a meeting at my house in the backyard once. I was always inspired by their writing and their enthusiasm to push their craft.

One night at the yellow house, one of the guys said he had created some music tracks to some of the poetry. We went into the garage behind the house where Robbie's makeshift studio was and listened to his music inspired by the poetry. I was in awe of this group. The music was complex yet catchy. I remember thinking this was what EDM (electronic dance music) aspired to be. It was musical and electronic at the same time. Robbie is now known as Robert DeLong, an EDM star, but I'm honored to have spent time with all of them.

## The Rock Star on the Porch

I spent a lot of time grading papers in my little office, looking out the window to see my rock-star neighbor sweeping his porch or organizing his garage. From my window I could see a surfboard, a mountain bike, and various cases for guitars and music equipment. Tim seemed to be constantly organizing and cleaning, often while on the phone or smoking a cigarette, and he became my sounding board, listening to my tales of woe at EVU with the attention and care of a therapist. I didn't know many other professional rock stars, but Tim seemed unusually insightful and curious about the world around him.

Talking to Tim about the rock-star life was fascinating, but he seemed genuinely curious about my life as an English professor at EVU. He had attended a Christian high school for a bit, and he was keenly aware of the role evangelicals were playing in politics. It didn't matter where we were—Puebla Tacos, Roscoe's Chicken and Waffles, on our porches, or backstage at one of his shows—Tim always seemed to enjoy talking and thinking about the world around him. Certainly, the space we were creating as friends seemed a million miles away from EVU. Whenever I needed a break from stressing about the maddening students or the stacks of papers to grade, I could always wander over to Tim's place to see what he was working on.

During winter break of 2007, Tim lamented that he'd gotten invites to several big celebrity New Year's parties. He generally didn't like such big scenes, and I could tell he felt some pressure to make appearances and do the rock-star thing because Sugarcult was at the height of its popularity. When New Year's Eve rolled around, I was preparing our house for our annual New Year's hang with family, friends, and some of the "bad" EVU profs. I told Tim to stop by for a New Year's toast before he headed out to his many parties, and he said he would.

From my side patio, we could see Tim in his garage, moving things around at around 9:00 p.m. He was still in his garage, dressed in black with a cool hat and boots. At 10:00 I wandered over to wish him Happy New Year, and he came back with me to say hi to Geri and the fifteen or twenty folks at my house, which included my brother and his family, some neighbors, and my EVU colleagues.

The EVU profs were in awe. They had heard my stories about hanging with Tim and all his rock 'n' roll exploits, and here he was. Seeing Tim interact with my nerdy professor friends was kind of amazing. For every question they asked him about his life, he asked one or two about their lives and their areas of academics. He had come over for a quick hello, but Tim sat down around the fire pit and made himself a part of the group. At 11:30, I asked him if he needed to get going to ring in the New Year at one of his big parties. He looked around at the group and sheepishly asked if it was okay if he just stayed with us.

The look on the faces of everyone was precious. The rock star was foregoing big Hollywood New Year's parties to hang with us.

Tim never made himself the center of attention, as one might assume a rock star would. He just became part of the group. When one of my colleagues started talking about his woodworking projects, both Tim and I perked up. We had talked at length about various projects we wanted to do in our houses and around our yards, and this guy had some serious power tools. Turned out, Tim was a nerd at heart just like us.

After the party, Tim told me he had a great time and that my friends seemed cool. I told him they were the "bad" ones. Like me. He had heard all about the shitty students and faculty at EVU, so he was surprised to meet my "bad" friends. All I could think was how excited my colleagues were to spend a New Year's Eve with a rock star.

I wondered if I could exist in the two worlds of EVU and my life on the outside. I would go on to bring my real-life friends and community into the EVU bubble in an attempt to do just that. But deep down, I knew.

## MY LIFE IN ONE PARTY

I threw a huge bash for my fortieth birthday in 2010. We rented a huge tent for the backyard, set up a stage for my musician friends to jam, and ordered a few kegs of beer and a few dozen bottles of wine. The 120 people who came were a beautiful representation of my life at that point. There were family and childhood friends, EVU students and colleagues, my musician friends from Midtones, and my inner circle of friends from Tuesday Night Café. At one point, the jam session included Keiko Agena playing drums, as she did in her role on *Gilmore Girls*; my friend, Jonathan, a killer session player, on bass; and Tim Pagnotta of Sugarcult singing and playing guitar with Quincy Surasmith, a leader of the TNC group. As they jammed through a couple of different covers, I smiled, knowing that they were the center of my life. EVU seemed a million miles away.

# 9

# The Straight Agenda

## ARCADIA, CALIFORNIA, 1988

At a party with my nerdy high school band geek and math club-type friends, we were watching a movie. We'd drunk soda, eaten junk food, and played board games. Wild party for sure. I hope my parents aren't reading this. A friend sat next to me and wrapped her arms around me.

"Why haven't you ever made a move?" she asked.

I was stunned. I mumbled something about my faith and saving myself for marriage, and I was vaguely aware that I was speaking unintelligibly.

"Let's go into that bedroom, and you can do whatever you want with me," she whispered in my ear, so our friends couldn't hear.

I don't regret not going into the room with my friend. She was, I later learned, going through a rough time of life with an emotionally abusive family and drama with friends at school. Having sex with her that night would have likely been life-changing and fun, but it could have just added to her trauma; so I am, to this day, glad I didn't take her up on her offer.

What I regret is how and why I turned her down, leaving her feeling rejected. I panicked and got up and went into the kitchen where I knew the parents of the house were, leaving my friend devastated on the couch. So many sermons and camp speakers ran through my mind, telling me that to give in to lust would be to sacrifice my purity and a good deal of my faith. Sensing my very salvation in the balance in the moment, I was literally terrified of what almost happened.

In a twisted way, I patted myself on the back for my response to my friend for many years. So deeply held was my faith that I turned down sex with a beautiful girl. I left out the part of me being terrified and fleeing to the safety of adults in the next room. The way I told the story for an embarrassing number of years, I portrayed myself as a warrior of God who could not be tempted by the desires of the flesh.

Until I met my wife. As we dated and got engaged, we told each other more and more about our lives, and while I had nothing to contribute when comparing past sexual experiences, I had that one story. To her credit, Geri was not impressed. To her, it sounded sad. I was honest and told her the real story. Through her eyes, I saw a scared, repressed boy fearful of the fires of hell instead of the godly warrior I had made myself out to be.

And of course, sex would be ever present at EVU. Christians are obsessed with sex.

## How Do I Seduce You?

The foreign student sauntered in, put her bag down, and sat across from me at my desk in my office.

"How do I seduce you?"

I laughed nervously, thinking this was some kind of joke, but she just stared at me, dead serious.

I thought back to that night in high school and laughed to myself. I was no longer afraid of hell or losing a chunk of myself in a sexual situation. What I was afraid of was being fired and damaging a young student's psyche. I calmly asked some questions clarifying her intentions, and quickly came to realize that her limited English was causing the misunderstanding. Mostly.

She was definitely flirting with me, but she was not asking how to literally seduce me. She wanted me to pay attention to her in an inappropriate way, for sure, but . . . whew.

I called my wife as soon as the student left my office and I might have bragged a little that a lovely young student had tried to seduce me, but that I had politely declined.

The student was more "worldly" than the typical EVU women, and I had to laugh when she showed up to class one morning in a tiny, tight-fitting club dress. A classmate who lived on her floor watched her sit down and said, "Nope. No, no, no," and dragged her back to their dorm to change into something more EVU-like. The student in the dress looked sincerely confused, but she came back in a loose T-shirt and jeans to the satisfaction of the class.

# Do Not Think About Sex, Sex, Sex, or Sex!

Other than money, nothing has a greater influence on day-to-day policy and interactions at EVU than sex. Especially gay sex. Most of the rules in the living areas, the rules of student conduct, and the rules establishing appropriate faculty-student interactions are because of the lurking potential for sex. Granted, so much of society is built around sex that it is no surprise that a place like EVU would be mindful of its existence and its temptations.

But, really.

Evangelical culture has the unhealthy fetishization of the human body and the criminalization of any semblance of healthy sexual life down cold. They have it nailed, so to speak.

To give a sense of evangelical views on sex, about a month before Geri and I got married, my dad handed us a book. He said it had really helped his marriage with my mom, and he wished he had had such sage Christian advice when they had gotten married. In it were revolutionary nuggets of marital wisdom informing the would-be marital partners that communication was important, finances were important, and sex was something the man wanted all the time, so the woman had to give it up, take one for the team, make a sacrifice for the good of the marriage. The man needs this, after all, and it is his for the taking as head of the biblical household. We laughed so hard as we skimmed that chapter that we actually shed tears. Throughout the chapter there was an underlying assumption that women didn't really want sex themselves. This was the man's domain. But it was absolutely the woman's role to submit, as the Bible commands, to her husband's desires. Outside of a close marital bond being established, though, there wasn't much in it for the woman. Typical.

This may seem an antiquated view of sexual dynamics between men and women in the twenty-first century, but it is part of the completely unhealthy and contradictory views of sexuality most evangelicals hold. On one hand, women aren't supposed to want sex, or rather, they aren't supposed to want sexual pleasure for themselves. They are supposed to want sex to please their husbands, though. It's somehow ungodly or unholy for a woman to desire sexual pleasure. This view is pervasive in the writings and teachings of evangelical Christianity. Even when I was growing up, the message was that men are buckets of lust that need to be beaten into holy submission. It's an all-encompassing endeavor to tame the savage sexual beast that lurks within us. The girls are taught a similar lesson of sex being the worst possible thing a woman can do, but the difference is that they aren't supposed to want it. There is even an assumption that they don't, and it's somehow unnatural for a woman to have a healthy sex drive. This is how we get those fucked-up concepts of Christian women needing to seek Jesus as their primary male companion.

I've heard so many women at EVU talk about Jesus as the greatest man they'll ever know or love. Loving him and being in relationship with Jesus is some kind of precursor to or a substitute for romantic love with their one and only (other than Jesus), the man they will marry. This leads to some really awkward statements. "I'm so in love with Jesus, I don't even want a boyfriend," or, "Jesus is the only man I need right now." I once made an entire class angry when I asked if Jesus was good at calling women back. I guess it wasn't that funny. Also, I never heard a male say the equivalent, "I don't need a girlfriend; I have Jesus."

And certainly, a cursory glance at lyrics to praise songs about Jesus helps to explain this sexual fascination with the savior. Lyrics describing Jesus "entering" us or "having his way with us" dominate the praise landscape. It doesn't take much imagination to view these lyrics through a perverted adolescent lens. Imagine all the talk of denying sex and then going to chapel to sing the words, "Lord, have your way in me."

Not sure if that would be considered sublimation or manifestation. Don't think about that one for too long, though.

Paging: Beavis and Butthead. Beavis and Butthead to the page . . .

One of my favorite songs I used to lead in InterVarsity Christian Fellowship was "Ain't Nobody Love Me Like Jesus." A visiting Black pastor informed me that this was the "honkified" version of the song. The original words were, "Cain't nobody do me like Jesus." Go ahead and let your inner teenager contemplate the weirdness therein.

Several well-known Christian books for students advise young couples not to pray together or sing worship songs together alone. The prevailing wisdom is that this intimate spiritual fervor leads directly to sexual temptation . . . or just sex. Or both. I used to think this was counterintuitive. How could doing something that brings people closer to God be a slippery slope (if they're doing it right, anyway) to sexual degradation? If this were true, there would naturally be the assumption that something was evil or sinful about prayer or worship. But now it makes sense to me, especially with the lyrics being what they are, and the spiritual fervor that can consume people who are deep in prayer. Sex, at its best, is a journey into an erotic state of consciousness, hence the often ridiculous faces we make when we orgasm (that's not just me, right?). If there can be a thin line between love and hate, there certainly could be a thin line between spiritual and sexual ecstasy. It could also help to explain Jim and Tammy Faye Baker.

So, take a normal sexual drive that a woman has and sublimate that into a spiritual relationship with Jesus, and you get a really damaged woman who thinks sex is evil and boys are to be desired but physically shunned. Now, take that same woman and give her a boyfriend, fiancé, and eventually a husband. All through the dating or courtship process, sex is out of the question. And let's say, for argument's sake, that they don't have sex. At all. As the Lord commands. They don't have sex because it's dirty and bad and wrong. Then they get married. Now sex is supposed to be a wonderful bond, and if they read the same book Geri and I read, a marital obligation to serve a husband's natural and rightful need. How the hell is a woman who has spent her entire life living chaste—because sex is the worst possible thing she could ever imagine doing—supposed to now have a healthy view of sex with her husband? Especially since it's still assumed that she doesn't get much out of sex outside of the satisfaction that she is being a good wife.

I personally know three couples who experienced weeping and sadness on their wedding nights, and I have heard anecdotally of countless more. It's a real problem. No wonder books have to continue to be written reminding women of their submissive duties to the marriage. Blessed are they.

You would think with all this negative programming built into evangelical culture, rigorous rules would not be necessary. But you would, naturally, be wrong. Despite all the evangelical programming the women receive, schools like EVU still feel it necessary to write and enforce the rules of engagement between the sexes. And quite naturally, the rules do not work. Sex happens and happens often at EVU. Oh, it may not happen with the regularity it does in secular schools with their coed dorms and Greek systems built around sex and debauchery. But it happens a lot more than the board of trustees would ever care to know. I know this because students used to tell me.

The rules are hardly enforced with any uniformity. If a regular, tuition-paying student were to be caught having sex, he or she would begin a process of rehabilitation. Repeat offenses would result in expulsion. It's all in the handbook. But, if, say, you are the daughter of prominent missionaries who are friends with some people on the board of trustees, you almost can't get kicked out. Remember my former student?

Sex is so criminalized at places like EVU, it's not even allowed for married people who happen to go there. You read that right. One of my students needed a prescription for birth control pills to help control her hormones because of migraines. There is a student health center at EVU, and they have birth control. But even with the medical diagnosis and the nonsexual reasons for her prescription, she had to sign a stack of papers promising she would not engage in premarital sex, and she had to have a one-on-one counseling session with the head nurse reinforcing the school's no-sex rules. And then she and her boyfriend decided to get married before their senior year. This complicated matters significantly and actually made their lives worse. The rules and overall ethos of the school criminalize sex so deeply that there is no married student housing on campus—because married people might have sex in EVU housing. Because of this sexual loophole, the couple found themselves without a place to live because the dorms and all the many apartment complexes owned by the school do not allow coed cohabitation, even to married couples. The only reason they were given? Sex. What would the other inhabitants, or students, say or think having neighbors who were potentially having sex? We'll never have the answer to this question, because the policy still stands. If only the school knew exactly how much sex was going on in those residences.

The couple had to find off-campus housing in the middle of the semester and couldn't find anything affordable in the area. It got so bad, one of the deans of students finally offered to let them stay in one of the apartment complexes near the end of the year, thereby making a grand exception to the "no sex on campus" rules. This after many of us on faculty demanded the school make amends for booting them out in the first place. To be fair, most of the people they encountered were sympathetic to their plight, but no one, until the very end, was willing to do anything about it. Rules were rules. And we know what happens when we break rules at EVU. Well, I do.

So, what were the rules? There were curfews established in all the living areas, limiting the hours students could be present in living quarters of the opposite sex. These rules were passionately and rigidly enforced by the resident advisers, and they were well-trained. Students often reported finding RAs lurking in the bushes outside of windows trying to catch students in violation of the curfew. Students were written up and given citations when caught. Of course, I can't tell you how many students have made the observation that sex can happen at any time of day in those living quarters. Keeping boys out of the girls' apartments between the hours of 10:00 p.m. and 7:00 a.m. will not keep willing partners from having sex. Students found ways to violate the curfew, or they just had sex during the day. College students. Smart kids.

Students often told me that the oppressive rules and the thrill of breaking them made sex even better for them, so, in a way, the rules did not have the effect they were intended to have. There's nothing like giving in to sexual desire, coupled with the thrill of breaking a sacred rule and the possibility of being caught, to stoke the fires of sexual adventure.

I'll let you in on a well-known secret. At any evangelical school, watch the entrances to the living areas during chapel. Two to three times each week, depending on the school's chapel schedule, you'll find students sneaking in to have sex in the dorms and on-campus apartments during chapel. It's the perfect time, really. The housing areas are basically empty, and the forty minutes or so of privacy gives easily thirty-five minutes more than the typical college boy needs to desecrate himself and his salvation.

I've mentioned that every year, for at least the last ten I was at EVU, I would ask students if they knew what sex was whenever anything remotely sexual came up in conversation. I would stop, midsentence, and say, "Oh, sorry. Do you all know what 'sex' is?" It was funny for the first couple of months of any semester, but it was always funny to me. I knew that, outside of a few "wild" students, they did not know what sex was. And what little they did know was inaccurate or just wrong.

Let's say a few knew the basic technical, biological concepts of sexual intercourse or human reproduction. The boys knew they had hormones raging through their bodies and that they couldn't wait to get married and have sex all day every day. That's exactly what most of them would say. All day, every day. The look on the women's faces was priceless. It was usually a mix of fear and confusion. Students experienced fear on a number of levels. Women weren't supposed to desire sex, so there was probably a worry about not appearing to come close to matching the eagerness demonstrated by the boys. Also, a lot of women in Christian settings just do not know a whole lot about sex, outside of the technical. But the boys had been educated on guilt-ridden, furtive glances at porn and the fetishizing descriptions of sex in Christian books. So they knew a little bit, but it's like that saying, "A little knowledge is a dangerous thing." It's not so much a dangerous thing as it is a pathetically clueless thing. Woe is the woman who knows a lot about sex at EVU. Certainly, having sex will bring judgment and hatred upon a woman, but even knowing about sex or knowing too many people who have sex can bring equal scorn and shame. This is a place where a student could and did make the claim, "If you watch ten pornos, it's the same thing as losing your virginity." So, using this logic, it's not hard to imagine people equating sexual experience with sexual knowledge. It's also hard not to laugh out loud at all of this.

Despite the potential for laughs, friendships ended before my eyes because of sex. Two girls in a freshman writing class had become good friends during orientation. They came to class together and always left together to go to chapel. Their social media profiles were filled with pictures together with Bible verses and proclamations of Christian friendship. And then we talked about the topic of sex for an argument paper, and one of the girls admitted she had had sex with an ex-boy-friend. Her friend turned in her seat, her mouth agape, with eyes filled with shock and disappointment. "You did?" she gasped. It was heart-breaking to watch. One girl looked guilty and ashamed. The other looked angry and hurt. Over the next few days, they stopped sitting together. They were not really friends by the end of the semester.

For some evangelical women, sex is the ultimate deal-breaker. Everything can be lost. Friendship, respect, and even salvation can hang in the balance of an evangelical woman's decision to explore her sexu-ality. So, for the most part, most play it safe and learn almost nothing about their sexuality with themselves or with a partner. And these poor women enter dating or courtship and then marriage with no developed sense of self, a guilt-ridden perspective of sex, and almost no chance of ever enjoying sex in their lifetimes. But it's not all their fault.

# The Boys Are Not Okay

For most good evangelical boys at EVU, sex is their penis being allowed to take center stage at a worship service where the wife joyously and piously does to it everything he wants her to as an expression of her admiration, love, and desire for him and for Jesus. And his penis. Mostly his penis.

There are countless examples of how I intuit this notion about penises, but the most telling is a conversation that took place several times in the classroom through the years. Inevitably, the topic of homosexuality would come up. The students would make appropriate faces of distaste or disgust, as any good evangelical should. Students would remark at the sin or the depravity or just the grossness of the idea of being sexual with a person of the same sex. A precious boy with a furrowed brow would raise his hand.

"I don't get it," several boys have said with complete sincerity. "How can two ladies, like, have sex? There's no man. So, there's no . . . you know . . . man parts."

Some of the boys would nod in agreement, and it would become instantly clear just who had watched porn and who had not. Some boys and women would look incredulous, as any normal person would. The question was layered with male-centric narcissism, the penis, and ignorance. In these boys' minds, sex was only possible if a penis—their penis, really—was present and given top priority. Without their penis, how can two women have sex?

One year when this tragic notion was shared by another clueless freshman boy, a tattooed female student turned around and said, "I feel so bad for whoever you marry." I wanted to high-five her, but I resisted. I just nodded at her and gave her a thumbs up.

The boys innocently shrugged. They had no idea what she was talking about. The tragic lack of knowledge and imagination these boys had about sex made me wonder if this was why the divorce rate for self-described Christians—as it's commonly stated—is higher than the national average.

In my Freshman Writing Seminars, I usually had an open assignment where students could choose any topic they wanted (approved by me, of course) where they could apply what they had learned in the class about argumentation. I would not allow them to write about abortion because I had never read a student paper on the topic, on either side, that could ever pass a basic composition course. But, so long as there was a suitable argument to be made both for and against the topic, they could do any paper they wanted.

Naturally, the most popular topic was about sex before marriage. I sometimes suggested it, but I usually didn't have to. So curious were these innocent eighteen-year-old kids to find out what the Bible really said, that usually at least one or two students came up with the topic themselves. What better place to do so than in an institution of higher learning? Almost always, the student would want to argue against sex before marriage. I gave them the chance to write arguments that were contrary to what they personally believed as an exercise in argumentation. This worked really well in political topics and all manner of social topics like drinking or dancing. So, if a student wanted to write a paper about sex and what the Bible said, the first task was always to establish what the Bible does say. Turns out, it says almost nothing about sex before marriage.

In fact, thanks to books like *Unprotected Texts* by Jennifer Wright Knust, a pastor and professor at Yale, we learn that there are actually plenty of stories that describe and even some that promote sex before marriage. Students came in fully confident that there are several crystal-clear verses that prohibit sex before marriage because that is what they were taught in no uncertain terms. But when they actually looked for them, they were left with a few vague references to a pure marriage bed or sexual purity in which cases the context didn't apply to a dating scenario. This is usually understood to be a result of the fact that there was no "dating" in the Bible. There were short "courtships," but those often amounted to having sex to seal the deal in some kind of marriage.

Bringing actual biblical analysis and theology to the discussion of human sexuality shines a cruel light on the views of the evangelical youth of today. Every year, a new group of kids came to my class saying things like: "If you masturbate X number of times, you lose your virginity." "If you watch X number of pornos, you're not a virgin anymore." "Your virginity is the greatest gift you could ever give your spouse."

That last one got me into some trouble. When I knew my days were numbered at EVU, I once responded to the "greatest gift" claim by saying I could think of better gifts. Power tools came to mind. A computer. Maybe an Xbox. I also compared the gift of virginity to giving someone a star to be named after him or her. It's a nice gesture, but in the world of gift-giving, there are much better options. Unless, of course, you are of the opinion that virginity before marriage is of the utmost demands from God, as told by the Bible. Which it clearly is not. In the last few years of my time at EVU, I made it a point to address this concept whenever it came up. It became a bit I did to see which kids had a sense of humor. The icy stares I got when I got to the words "power tools" sustained me and my dark cynicism to the end. I knew someone in those classes was writing this down to report to the school.

And yet, even with such a lack of clarity, deeply ingrained indoctrination always makes up for intellectual confusion. What I'm saying is that even without clear biblical guidelines, the teachings of youth and high school pastors are not easily unseated from a young evangelical mind.

"Would you marry someone who wasn't a virgin?" a boy asked the class. He was a member of that worst section of Freshman Writing Seminar who I mentioned before. His question was a rhetorical grenade in that class.

"No way!" shouted most of the boys. The rest of the class seemed to be deep in thought. It was not an easy question for them. They were killing themselves to tamp down all evidence of their own sexuality. The idea that their future spouse, a person whom God himself had already chosen for them, was not taking their virginity as seriously as they were seemed to be just too much to think about. And one or two of them had already had sex, so the question was personal for them.

I should note that in each of these scenarios, there were usually one or two "normal" students who were just as shocked and amused by these discussions as I was. We would look at each other in silent solidarity, knowingly nodding our agreement that these kids were pretty gosh darn fucked up.

I added more troubling information to the question.

I told the boys that this was the most beautiful woman they had ever met, and it was crystal clear that God had brought this woman into their life. She was godly, righteous, and was crazy about you. You wouldn't marry her just because she wasn't a virgin?

This knocked a few of the boys off their self-righteous mounts. But one boy, a wealthy son of a professional golfer, was resolute. I mentioned him previously, but this attitude is worth revisiting.

"No. I'm not marrying some skank," he said with righteous conviction. The word rolled off his tongue so naturally, and most of the class accepted it wholeheartedly, with most nodding their approval. Only a few of us winced at the stark misogyny and patriarchy on display.

The wildly unpredictable woman in the class chimed in with her usual demented wisdom. She said that having sex before marriage destroys any chance that the marriage will be fulfilling. It was a fact, she said.

As this was near the end of my days at EVU, I decided to double down on the teachable moment. I told her, fixing my gaze directly upon her, that my wife had lived a fairly wild life before she had become a Christian and that she was not a virgin when we started dating. And yet, I felt we had the greatest marriage I could ever imagine. Was this student really saying my marriage was somehow cursed or less than amazing?

She thought about it for a second—and it was a real thought too. She took a deep breath, looked me right back in the eye, and said, "Yes. Your marriage is not what it should be."

The class gasped. She had said some crazy shit before, but here she was telling her professor that his marriage was irreparably damaged by his wife's promiscuity.

I wasn't even mad. I was in awe of her courage and her steadfast commitment to her beliefs, however odd and contrived they might be. I was a little shocked. And yet, I wasn't.

This is how evangelicals view sex and marriage. It is dangerous to society and to women. These people are not okay.

## AND NOW FOR SOMETHING COMPLETELY FORBIDDEN . . .

I bring up all this talk of fucked-up heteronormative sexuality to bring this book to a close with the "issue" that would be my undoing at EVU: homosexuality. I didn't say LGBTQIA on purpose because in the 2010s, just the notion of same-sex anything caused heads to explode. Until Donovan Ackley came out as trans in 2013 and made national news, the school likely had no concept of anything to do with trans or nonbinary identities, much less asexuality, pansexuality, and so on. Honestly, it still doesn't.

I acknowledge I'm writing from a place of privilege as a cishet male, even an Asian American one. For whatever risks I took in supporting LGBTQIA students, those who actually were LGBTQIA had so much more to lose. And in evangelical culture, they have so much less to gain. There is no way forward with full inclusion or full acceptance in evangelical spaces. Just as there is no way for me, a Japanese American with decent taste in music.

In the early 2000s, I gave hints that I was affirming and inclusive in my faith. I never said anything negative about queer people when the topic came up. I spoke often of my queer friends, and I praised them as people. And I never allowed any kind of bigotry in any class discussion. Occasionally, students came out to me or "confessed" their struggles with homosexuality, and I would encourage them to find inclusive spaces. In most cases, I was the only person they could talk to.

As time went on, and after I left the faith, I grew bolder in expressing my views. The "issue" of homosexuality and the Bible was one I had spent fifteen years on before this. When my wife and I started dating, we recognized the dilemma of queerness and our faith. We decided to embark on a personal Bible study looking at all the passages that mentioned homosexuality. We were on the fence about the issue before we did this study, willing to concede to whatever the Bible "really" said. But after we were done with the commentaries, concordances, and references, we were sure the Bible really said nothing about contemporary issues like homosexuality. In the same way the role of women can be contextualized to match today's culture, or how brutal rules about keeping the Sabbath are completely ignored, the matter of homosexuality seemed to fall in a similar category. At the very least, it was not a clear-cut issue. We were twenty when we did this study, and lives enriched by our queer friends only served to further our deconstruction from any kind of fundamentalist faith.

During one of the weeks when parents are invited to visit our classrooms, I gave my regular lecture on Flannery O'Connor. The parents seemed interested and smiled at my humorous or sarcastic remarks at the "old South" with its racism and backward ways. Then at the end of the class I listed all the stories that would be covered on the exam the following week. One student raised her hand and asked about one of the stories, "The Two," by Gloria Naylor. I reminded the class that "The Two" was the story about the lesbian couple and how they lived in the building with others in the Black community outside of Chicago. Everyone, of course, remembered the story. During that lecture we discussed a Christian's response to having a gay or lesbian neighbor. I tried to steer the class toward the idea that Christians can be good, loving neighbors to those who might live in ways they disagree with. Almost everyone in the class agreed with that. As I reminded the class that we had decided that we liked the characters and actually could be their neighbors, one set of parents quickly gathered their things and stormed out of the room. I finished my review, and the class ended.

I didn't think much of the parents leaving. Parents often came and went during these weeks, often leaving early to get to another class or to attend a meeting organized by the school. But they didn't usually leave in such a furious manner. The mom glanced at me as she exited. I knew that look well. It said, "You are a horrible person. How dare you!"

The next week I got an email from my department chair asking me to come see him. I couldn't think of anything I had said or done in the last couple of months to get me into trouble. I had even joked with some colleagues that I might have been losing my edge, as I had learned how to give my lectures and lead my discussions without driving my students into a righteous rage.

I sat down in my department chair's office, my usual seat to the left of his desk, and heard him tell me that the dean, again, wanted some "clarification" on some things. My poor department chair. He always looked out for me, and I think it grieved him to have to constantly bring me in to account for what was often nothing. This one was serious, and the dean had wanted to talk to me directly, but my chair had stepped in and promised to talk to me himself. Apparently, the dean snapped, "Talk to him." Nice guy.

My boss read an email from one of the old, White, crotchety biology professors I often end up sitting near at the lunch table in the cafeteria, whom we both knew well. The email had been sent to directly to the dean—not to me, and not to my boss, which bothered us both. According to the email, the parents who had stormed out of my classroom went directly to a barbecue hosted by the biology department and vented to my crotchety colleague that they had just come from an English class where the professor was openly and blatantly promoting the "gay agenda." Now, a professor at any school, upon hearing such a charge about a colleague, would likely ask some follow-up questions. Such a professor might inquire about what words or actions, exactly, had given such an impression. A deeper soul might ask about the context of said words or actions. And then there is always the option of going directly to the professor in question for clarification, since you often have lunch with him and were even assigned to him as a mentor when said professor went through new-faculty orientation. But my crotchety colleague did none of these things. He just sent a long, angry email to the dean of the school demanding action be taken, with the not-so-subtle hint at firing me because I was unfit to be a professor at EVU. If he had taken any of the prior steps, he would have learned that my "promoting the gay agenda" amounted to listing off a story the class had read and using the words *lesbian* and *Christian love* in the same sentence.

I explained this to my department chair, and he was not surprised. But I had to strike back at my crotchety colleague. "You should know," I said as I got up to leave. "He (the crotchety colleague) begins every semester by going through his biology syllabus and then saying, 'If this is too hard, then go be an English major.'" I had confirmed this fact over several years, asking students in his class if he said this on the first day. It happened in every class he taught. It was part of his canned introductory lecture. As I left my department chair's office, he was composing an angry email of his own. It was petty of me to throw my crotchety colleague under the bus, but I had been waiting for the right time to do so for a while, and this seemed as good a time as any. Accuse me of promoting the gay agenda? Ha. I expose you for being an asshole. At a Christian university, one might feel compelled to turn the other cheek or forgive seventy times seven times, but I was no longer a Christian, and it felt great to hit back.

It was time to actually promote the "gay agenda," which turns out to be less exciting than evangelicals imagine. The agenda? To live and thrive like anyone else.

By the time some students decided to start a secret Gay/Straight Alliance at EVU, I knew for certain a reckoning was coming. I don't know if I was the first faculty to be asked to be involved, but I was honored. Despite my strong feelings, though, my decision to get involved was not as easy as it might have seemed.

There were very real consequences for anyone who was caught even supporting LGBTQIA issues, much less being LGBTQIA-identified. The school had not-so-subtly fired a couple of professors for being gay. It had expelled students and outed them to their families and communities. And I'd listened outside of enough open doors to classes with professors who made jokes about gay people, or worse, promoted hatred against gay people.

For some context, Abbie Cirelli, whom I mentioned earlier as the writer for the *EVU Tribune*, was a freshman in 2007, and she witnessed the first ever protest for gay rights at EVU. Some students wore tape on their mouths and held signs that said they were being silenced by EVU because two students were given the draconian choice to renounce their identities or leave. At the time, Abbie wasn't sure what to think about homosexuality. She was a fervent evangelical, but she also took to heart the teachings of Jesus about love. By 2009, she was completely fed up with evangelical Christianity and decided to do what she could to fight back against all oppression at the school. In addition to getting involved in feminist movements on campus, Abbie collaborated with two other students, including Latin American Student Association founder Matthew Gonzalez, to start an underground support group for gay students. This was before the days of trans and nonbinary inclusion, so they called the group the Gay/Straight Alliance, or GSA.

Matt and Abbie told me about their plans, and they asked if I would be involved. I asked for a day or two to respond. It occurred to me that this was a reckoning of sorts. A part of me felt that I could remain at EVU, doing what I was doing, supporting the BIPOC and LGBTQIA students and teaching English. A number of my friends reminded me of what was at stake for those students to have professors like me actively involved at the school. I took every part of my job seriously, dedicating myself to helping students learn and grow as people. But I also knew that an organization of LGBTQIA students, however secret or underground, needed support, and giving support would come at a cost. If this group were going to grow to hold events, it would eventually be found out, and I would be found out if I were involved. I already had a reputation. But the school had a history of ignoring behaviors as long as I was discreet. If I wanted to make teaching at EVU a career, I would have to play by the rules, which, granted, I had not done very well. In addition to not lending my time and energy to forbidden underground LGBTQIA groups, I would have to stop smoking weed with English majors, and I would have to cease offering extra credit on papers for using *fuck* in a creative but logical way to keep me awake while grading. I would have to stop making athletes drop out because I pointed out errancies in the Bible. I would have to reign in the MEP students from trying to foment revolution. I would have to become another boring, White-affirming, LGBTQIA-hating, sexist conservative. At least I would have to appear so at appropriate times.

All those things, except maybe the extra credit for *fuck* in papers, were nonstarters for me, and I knew it. I had built a ten-year career out of being myself, teaching the writing and literature I loved, and using those subjects to open students up to lives of love and peace. Despite the stress from dealing with evil students and colleagues, I slept well at night and woke up each morning looking forward to doing my part.

But I couldn't say no to the GSA.

It was around this time that I was selected by the students to be one of the faculty to speak in chapel. In my talk about how a poetic eye and perspective could be useful for Christian living, I mentioned how I wished nothing but abundance for my queer friends. I was told that was the first time in the history of the school that anyone referenced LGBTQIA people in a positive way. Students I knew and many I didn't walked up to me all week with tears in their eyes and hugged me. I got free coffee all week from a closeted barista. The need was always crystal clear, but the universe seemed to be telling me to actively do something to help the hurting LGBTQIA students at EVU.

The creation of the GSA forced me to choose a path I had the privilege to avoid before. Without the GSA I could just secretly support students who happened to be in my classes. But with an active group supporting students and planning subversive events, I felt like I had to help.

The leaders came up with a mission statement and a plan to keep the group safely away from the eyes and ears of the EVU staff and administration. I didn't get invited in until they had met a few times, establishing their ritual of reading the mission statement and having people give their "testimonies" about why they were there. I gave mine that first meeting, and my printed story was added to a folder of the members.

For the first year, they met in an on-campus apartment that belonged to Sammie Howell, the eventual leader of the Asian club, APASO. I arrived and was quickly ushered to a hushed group of students, most of whom I knew. There were students in student government, RAs, and Bible study leaders, kids who had visibility. All of us were taking a great risk to be there. As we planned the first event, an evening of poetry and music not unlike my beloved Tuesday Night Café, we discussed who could be let into the group. Anyone wishing to join would have to be vetted to ensure the secrecy of the group. If the Student Life staff had spies attend off-campus parties to catch students drinking, they would surely send spies to an illegal Gay/Straight Alliance. And yes, they did send spies to parties off campus.

That first year, we began a yearly tradition of boldly holding an on-campus event we named "Art Night." Through an *Oceans Eleven* level of planning, we used allies at every level of student government and staffing to reserve the outdoor amphitheater, get a PA, lights, and tables, and put on a queer-themed night of poetry and music. In broad view of the school.

All the Art Nights were special events with dozens of people in attendance at first and hundreds of people in attendance at its height within five years. I usually performed a poem or a song, joining the students in a brazen outpouring of support for our LGBTQIA community.

That first Art Night established a level of emotional catharsis and a standard of community presence that would last for the next seven or eight years. In total defiance of the oppressive school policies, we read tearful poems, sang heartfelt songs, and offered up a barrage of protests against the school and advocacy for our shared humanity, all right in the middle of campus.

The school would eventually kick the group off campus, but the Gay/Straight Alliance, then called Haven, just moved the event to the community college campus that was literally next door to EVU, in a parking lot adjacent to EVU's student parking lot. The school would essentially destroy the whole community by later reforming the group to become an official student organization that just ended up being a discussion group run by non-affirming EVU staff. But goddamn. What a run they had.

# I Felt a Cleaving in My Mind . . .

The more my TNC friends became my chosen family, the more they naturally integrated into my life at EVU. They listened to me describe APASO and its hopeless mission to drive awareness and alleviate some of the racist behavior. They were horrified to hear about how the queer kids were treated. Traci had fast become one of my closest friends, along with several others, and they each volunteered to come speak to APASO on weeknights. They practiced with me to play music at the annual APASO coffeehouse, and they came to my classes to share their passion for creativity.

Shin Kawasaki came to every event he could possibly come to. As one of the finest guitarists, singers, and all-around musicians I've ever met, he played at least five Multi-Ethnic Programs picnics at the beginning of the school year, he played at almost every APASO coffeehouse, and he came to speak at my literature classes. Keiko Agena, who was Shin's wife, came to every APASO coffeehouse she could, playing drums, singing, and just showing up to support. Jenny Yang, then a brand-new comedian, came to a few APASO coffeehouses, first as a singer with the bands I was playing with and then as a true working comic. Greg Watanabe, an acclaimed theater actor and cofounder of the 18 Mighty Mountain Warriors, an Asian American sketch comedy troupe, came to my creative writing classes to talk about the craft of writing. My own bandmates were always available to perform with me at the APASO coffeehouses. Dave, Grace, Paddy, and Jenny were all in Band Moto with me, and they came to play during my last years at EVU. Even an old childhood friend, Robert Gates, a Juilliard graduate in musicology and composition, jammed with me at a few APASO coffeehouses.

My new community reminded me every day of the sinister oppression in evangelical spaces, providing a haven for me to explore my identity and develop as a human being free from the radical fundamentalist person I used to be. Through their eyes, I saw EVU as a sinister place raising up the next generation of fundamentalist thought leaders and influencers who would criminalize the very existence of my friends.

At one of the last APASO coffeehouses, I brought traci and our friend Narinda, both nonbinary and queer, to perform a poetry round-robin we had been doing at different events, but that we had never done at EVU. It was also the first time the content of an APASO meeting was so openly queer. We brought our poetry notebooks up and had the audience suggest topics, to which we responded with our poems that related to the topics. The joke was always that I, the less-gifted, less-prolific poet, would just read the same few poems at every event, while traci and Narinda would dig deep into their collections and just kill it with their amazing poems. The audience shouted "love" as the first topic, and traci launched into a poem from her first book, *Signaling*, that wondered what it would have been like to have affirming family during her youth—a family who would ask if she had met any nice girls as often as they asked about boys. It was a sincere, melancholic poem that pointed out some of the experiences queer people need to unpack as they examine their journeys and the lives they hope to lead.

As traci read, I noticed some people at the back of the room waving at me, frantically. My phone started buzzing, and I saw that several of the other MEP leaders were texting me.

"Stop! Carl is freaking out!"

"Carl is threatening to shut the event down if you don't stop now!"

"Carl is having a cow! Stop!!!"

Carl was the head of the Student Life and, by extension, the MEP programs. He oversaw these events, and apparently he was not happy about queer poetry.

I stared at the texts and glanced at Narinda and traci, two of my closest friends in the world, and felt a chill go through me as I realized their very existence made evangelicals freak the fuck out. After traci finished her poem, there was wild applause from the MEP crowd, but I quickly pulled us off the stage. Narinda and traci were naturally confused, but I stared at them wide-eyed, tilting my head to the back of the room, communicating to them that we needed to stop.

The show went on without any other problems, and overall it was a beautiful night. Someone told me Carl needed to talk to me, but in the coming days I made it my mission to avoid him for as long as I could. I sat in meetings with him in the room, always sitting near the door, so I could flee as soon as the meeting concluded. I kept my eye out for him while walking around campus, even ducking into buildings or classrooms to avoid him. He finally cornered me in a hallway a few weeks later.

"Hey, Scott. So I've been meaning to ask you how you felt about the APASO coffeehouse."

*Fuck.* I told him it was a beautiful night, and he agreed.

"Yeah, totally. Awesome."

We stood awkwardly for a second, both of us knowing what needed to happen. And if I knew the guy like I think I did, he understood his role as Spanish Inquisitor was on the wrong side of history, but he had a job to do to protect his ass.

"Just so you know, when you guys pull stunts like that, I'm the one who catches hell for it," he said. It was classic. He was the victim here. A cishet White guy who shut down two queer women of color, basically criminalizing their very existence, was the victim.

I just shook my head as he explained that some changes were coming regarding the policies of the MEP organizations in light of our "stunt" and the prolific activism of LASA. Those may have been beautiful days for the MEP students, but they were numbered days. EVU was about to strike back.

# 10

# It's Their House (But It's Our World)

## ARCADIA, CALIFORNIA, MINI HIGH SCHOOL REUNION, 1993

As a recent college graduate, I was still a fairly strong Christian, but my deconstruction was well underway. At a friend's house in Arcadia, a group of us from high school got together to catch up. Included in this get-together were the friends who were part of a high school ministry I had been involved with, loosely affiliated with Campus Crusade, a college ministry like InterVarsity Christian Fellowship. The parents who had sponsored the group were there, and I felt uneasy around them because my own faith, however strong at the time, had radically shifted to be more inclusive of my gay friends.

At some point, I inevitably ended up chatting with those parents as they sat down where I was sitting. They asked about college and what my plans were, and I told them I was about to start teaching bilingual elementary school in the Bay Area. They seemed happy about that, noting the many opportunities to spread the good word. I tried not to visibly cringe. Something about these friendly, cheerful White people was making me uncomfortable. And then the mom made clear why.

"I'm still working at the hospital," she said smiling. She was a nurse, and I remembered my high school days hearing her tell stories about witnessing to the patients unfortunate enough to be in her care. But on this day she started talking about the hardest part of her job: AIDS patients. She said it broke her heart, but she refused to work with anyone with AIDS because God had judged them, and she could not go against God's judgment.

I immediately got angry and started yelling at her. It just came out. Everyone at the party looked over at our table as I accused her of bigotry and hate. Some friends invited me to come inside and cool down, and I went with them, leaving these callous parents sitting there looking sad. Of course, nothing I said made any difference to them.

But I came away from that day with a couple of revelations: (1) I would never speak to those people ever again, including their daughter who had been a friend of mine. Fuck those evil, bigoted people. (2) I noted how many of my friends were mad at me for causing a stir and laying into the older "good Christian" White folks. One friend told me I was too hard on them because they were "good people" I just didn't see eye to eye with. Fuck that. Even as a Christian, I made it a personal mission to fight against bigotry, even if that meant telling the world that Christians are not typically "good people." In fact, I was starting to realize that many Christians were pretty fucking (adverb) evil.

My time at EVU would eventually make me realize that non-evil Christians are the exception instead of the rule. The 2016 and 2020 presidential elections would show that the vast majority of Christians, because of their votes for Trump, are super fucking evil.

# TRUMP IS A MANIFESTATION OF EVANGELICALISM

As I look back at my time at EVU, I am not surprised Trump became president on the shoulders of evangelicals. It's one of the biggest ironies we've ever seen, because Mr. "Two Corinthians" is no practicing Christian of any stripe. Most of the world seemed to wonder how "good" Christians could possibly vote for a hateful, racist, sexist ignoramus, but it made perfect sense to me.

Business and capitalism are spiritual fruit in evangelical spaces, and Trump is an archangel . . . or a fruit store. In addition to criminalizing gay people's very existence and the healthy sexual identities and practices of everyone, the most important "value" of evangelicals is money. Money justifies every racist, sexist, homophobic, xenophobic word or action an evangelical has. I'm not saying money forgives actions motivated by these ideas. I'm saying it pays for them. From my view, money, and the drive to attain it, is the root of every base instinct of a fundamentalist evangelical today.

Until recently, the EVU bookstore sold a license-plate cover with the reference "Jeremiah 29:11" on it. The verse says, "For I know the plans I have for you, declares the LORD, plans to prosper you and not to harm you, plans to give you hope and a future." Or just look at the huge bestseller at the time, *The Prayer of Jabez*, which was about expanding your territory.

You don't have to look very hard to see overt nods to the money and power values of evangelicalism. God will make you prosperous if you are faithful. There were no license-plate covers with verses about love being the greatest commandment or forgiveness being necessary even to our enemies. Prosperity is the ultimate payoff for hating gay people, keeping women in their place, marginalizing and oppressing people of color, and criminalizing sex and sexuality.

These are the terms I use to spread the word that evangelicals are a real, present threat to the world. They would counter that their "values" are biblically founded and rooted in God's love, but tell that to the people who are harmed and oppressed. It sure doesn't feel like love.

Branding is just as important as scholarship at places like EVU. At my first faculty meeting, I was surprised to see about half of the faculty wearing crimson polo shirts with the school logo. They looked like employees at a red Walmart. One of my colleagues who did not share my disdain for the matching corporate shirts went around asking where he could get one. There were some female colleagues wearing the shirts, but it was mostly a male deal. As someone who aspired to be a great teacher at a university, I thought the shirts were embarrassing. I couldn't imagine professors at UCLA or Harvard wearing branded polos with the school logo.

I'll just say it. EVU is more Walmart and Chick fil A than university.

It was often discussed among faculty, quietly, that EVU was structured as a business instead of as a university. The product was a degree, and students were paying customers. I guess the professors were the shelf-stockers or cashiers. The ethos of the school drips with conservative values about financial success. Money is everything, despite the "God First" motto everywhere. In fact, "God First," in my opinion, really meant "Money First" at EVU. It was a transitive relationship. God=sustenance. Sustenance in our culture=money. Therefore, God=money.

Such a view has a name. It's called the prosperity gospel. Those old-time, late-night televangelists telling unwitting followers that God wants to bless them with untold riches, if only they would demonstrate their faithfulness by sending a fat check—those guys were the forefathers of the modern prosperity gospel. In short, the belief is that God wants to bless his followers with riches. So, if things are right in one's faith, he or she would naturally have a lot of money. Today's evangelical subscribes to a more subtle version of this gospel. It could be money that God bestows as blessings on his people. But it could be anything we want. Need a new car? New job? Healing from an illness? Prayers are used to claim these things in his name. Evangelicals are often told that God totally wants to bless you with these things you want and need, if only you would *let* him! Stop sinning! Pray every day! Read your Bible! Which could be confusing because the Bible would also provide a lot of theological examples that run contrary to this view. And, of course, when prayers don't get answered, the child dies, the job falls through, there is no puppy under the Christmas tree . . . it's God saying the timing isn't right. Or you just didn't read, pray, or live correctly. Either way, you're just fucked (adjective).

Most evangelicals subscribe to this unspoken and coded capitalism in some form, with varying degrees of severity. The School of Business at EVU proudly and openly promotes the prosperity gospel when it thinks no one is looking. I've heard business professors say things like, "What's wrong with making money?" to which Jesus might have something to say. Much like the White supremacists in this country who don't like being called White supremacists, most professors who teach in the School of Business get downright dodgy and deny supporting the prosperity gospel when the topic comes up. Of course, there are some who openly teach it and will proudly defend it.

One professor in the School of Business was briefly part of a group of us who gathered to play poker and drink. I asked him directly, "Does the School of Business endorse the prosperity gospel?" He awkwardly said he didn't think so. But maybe some did. After he engaged in some obfuscating and rambling about what he taught, I realized he had little or no idea what I was talking about. Someone else asked a follow-up question about the theological implications of capitalism, and he just froze. He looked like we had just asked him to explain the laws of thermodynamics. The guy was shook. And really lost. Or he was pretending to be. And he wasn't alone in the School of Business.

I had a student come into a class crying in one of my Introduction to Literature classes. She sat down and tried to compose herself just as I was beginning my lecture. After class, she was slow to gather her things, so I approached her and asked if she was okay. She started crying again and recounted how her business professor had just mocked her in front of the entire class. She had written a paper about how environmental concepts could be profitable and good for business in the long run. The professor, while handing back papers to the class, stopped at hers and announced to the class that they had a "tree hugger" in their midst. He went on to mock her and get laughs from the class, piling on about her "liberal" views to the delight of the students. The sad irony was that this student was not a liberal. She saw herself as a conservative. At least she did until that class. And naturally, that class was called Business Ethics.

At some point, the Western Association of Schools and Colleges, WASC, must have informed EVU's School of Business that they needed to offer a class called Business Ethics. But, as with most schools, I'm sure, ethics are detrimental to good business (or good evangelicalism). EVU is really no different from a lot of business schools, I'm sure. You have to make money. The ends justify the means. After all, if God is money, the pursuit of money is a holy endeavor. There can be no higher calling.

I knew the daughter of the dean of the School of Business was in my class, but I never imagined that I would come to be reviled by the entire School of Business.

Before class one day, a student who had me in Freshman Writing Seminar sat down and told me she had very bad news to report: she had become a business major. It was an inside joke from the previous semester. We had talked about the evils of money, as stated in the Bible, and I had joked that, based on a few different verses, one could not be a Christian and a business major. I can't emphasize enough just how much we were kidding when we arrived at this thought. And the joke continued on this particular day. It was before class started, and I reminded the student of the sin of "usury." Making money with money, especially through unfair interest rates on loans, was considered a grave sin until relatively recent times. I had taught a Shakespeare class and discovered that one of the famous Shakespeare signatures featured on T-shirts and mugs was found in a court document regarding a case where his father had been convicted of usury, and Shakespeare was testifying on his behalf. So, I half-jokingly brought up the funny little fact that devout Christians from Shakespeare's day would have thought the entire School of Business was heretical (pretty much how they—as evangelicals—should perhaps consider it in the present day). The idea of teaching Christians to operate in a capitalistic society where interest and markets drove everything would have been pretty darn evil in their eyes. But the kicker that fateful day was that I said to the student, "Well, I guess you're going to hell now. Along with the English majors." We all laughed, and I explained our joke to the rest of the class as students continued to come in. And everyone did laugh. No one misunderstood the joke. No one called the president or my boss to complain. It was all good.

The daughter of the dean of the School of Business had thought the whole discussion was particularly funny and even interesting. She went downstairs to the office of the School of Business and said hi to her mom, the dean, recounting with her friends the humorous exchange they had heard before my class. The dean did not find the joking to be humorous at all. I found out a day later that she immediately fired off an angry email to my dean in the College of Liberal Arts and Sciences, demanding I apologize or be fired.

I was summoned to my usual corner in the office of my English department chair to answer to the accusation that I had told business majors they were going to hell. My chair looked baffled as he read the email. He was accustomed to hearing complaints about me, but this seemed extreme. Even for me.

He smiled sadly, saying he thought he knew what the story was, but he was instructed to get my story. I told him about the humorous conversation, even asking if I was also in trouble for saying English majors were also going to hell. He just shook his head and lamented the sad state of affairs at EVU.

The interim provost once told a group of professors not to use satirical humor in our classrooms because students don't always understand the humor, and this can cause trouble. I knew this lack of both intellect and humor to be true at EVU, but I didn't agree it should necessarily lead to trouble. I actually increased my use of satirical humor after the provost said these words. If I were to teach students about language and its uses, satire had to be part of it. Even if their faith made them incapable of understanding it.

My chair said he would explain the situation to the liberal arts dean, and I left his office with him shaking his head at the absurdity of it all. Later, I was in line at the school coffee shop when the School of Liberal Arts and Sciences dean walked in and stood in line behind me. I apologized to him for the misunderstanding and told him about the conversation. I actually had him laughing out loud in the coffee shop at my recounting of the incident. I remind you, here, that I can be very funny. Still no accent, right? He said he figured that was the case but had to respect the dean of the School of Business and her feelings on the matter.

The dean of the School of Business had heard secondhand a humorous conversation that took place before class. She did not find it to be humorous, but instead of contacting me directly to confront me, she wrote an angry email to the dean of liberal arts and sciences. And she made some demands. I was to apologize to the class for besmirching the good name of business majors and the School of Business, and I was to schedule a meeting to explain myself to the student business club. I agreed to do these things only because I wanted to keep the English department out of trouble.

Throughout my time at EVU, the only thing I really regretted about my troubles was the fact that it caused the English department trouble. A few years later, during my last year, when I was being repeatedly confronted about my views of LGBTQIA issues, my chair told me directly that the department would go to great lengths to protect students, but it could not and would not protect faculty. That year there was an openly gay English major who won a major award at the National English Honor Society conference. This was huge for him and for the school. Naturally, the school inquired into the matter, asking the department to hide the sexuality of the student, but he had written an essay specifically about being gay. The department, including most of my colleagues, stood by him. I was no longer a member of the department at this point because I had been demoted to entry-level adjunct by then, but I was especially proud of the English department. But, however noble this stand, there was nothing anyone was going to do to stand with me against homophobia.

I half-jokingly asked my chair if the reason they could support the openly gay student but not the LGBTQIA-allied professor was because EVU considers students to be paying customers and the faculty to be financial liabilities. He laughed heartily. But he didn't say no.

I never met with the dean of the School of Business. I know some alumni and faculty there, so I asked them about her. They told me she was a wealthy woman who lived in South Orange County, and she was extremely conservative. Obviously. The School of Business is an interesting study in the bizarre cognitive dissonance necessary to run an accredited evangelical university. Most churches could come up with dozens of ways business in America is completely contrary to the teachings of Jesus. Whether one brings up issues of stewardship, greed, usury, the story of Jesus overturning the money-changers' tables, the camel getting through the figurative eye of the needle, several parables, turning the other cheek, being generous, the parable of the widow's mite, or just the idea of the meek inheriting the earth, it's not hard to come to the conclusion that the way we do business in America is highly problematic. With corporations and profit-driven everything, an entire School of Business at an evangelical school whose motto is "God First" would obviously have to justify its existence by doing some biblical gymnastics to explain how it answers to those biblical examples, among many others. But no. No gymnastics, mental or physical, are performed. The prosperity gospel is so foundational to evangelical culture, it is simply assumed to be theological truth.

Take the Business Ethics course mentioned earlier. A friend of mine who usually teaches philosophy was asked to teach this class once. He approached it from a classic ethics perspective, having students read philosophy and morality texts. In other words, he was showing clear arguments about ethical behavior like any ethicist would. But the students hated it, and the School of Business was not pleased. Apparently, the actual topic of ethics had never been addressed when this course was put into the curriculum to appease WASC for accreditation. For EVU business majors, the course was seen as a primer on how to avoid the violations of ethical standards while maximizing profits. This explains the harrowing experience of my crying student who was humiliated by her professor for daring to write a paper about environmental issues in business. She was foolish enough to actually try to bring, oh, what's it called, oh, right, "ethics" into her research.

My colleague from philosophy was never again asked to teach the course. And when I met with the president and vice president of the student business club, as I was required to do, they were shocked to hear me argue that issues of their faith don't always square up with the common business practices of the day. Shocked! They met me at the coffee shop on the main campus, dressed in business-casual attire with requisite matching polos, all puffed up with righteous indignation. They immediately stated that they wanted me to explain my joke about business (and English) majors and how I could say such a hurtful, groundless thing. Instead of being defensive, I went on the offensive.

No punkass business majors in sensible polos and khakis were going to intimidate me. I explained to them about the history of usury and brought up several examples of Jesus' teaching that seemed to contradict a pro-business mode of thinking. I told them I did not apologize for bringing the issue up, whether in casual conversation or in my lectures and class discussions. I asked them how they answered to such issues in their classes and in their club meetings.

They were silent at first. Then they reached for their business jargon to try and obfuscate the matter, saying Jesus was not anti-business and something about God being able to use business for his glory, but I held them to my point. Finally, the president admitted that he had never discussed anything I had brought up in any class. Ever. He was a graduating senior. I asked if any professor of any business class had ever mentioned the obvious contradictions between the teachings of Jesus and the business practices in a capitalistic society. He told me no professor had ever brought any of this up, but he wished they had. The vice president, a young woman, dressed in the same way, nodded her head.

Now I almost felt bad. I wanted to hit them hard with some truth, but outside of the safety of my classroom where these discussions are built on community trust and relationship, I was simply some angry, old, and probably foreign Asian dude handing two White kids their assess on a gilded platter. I could have gloated, and part of me almost wishes I did. But I just felt bad for them. They were sadly misguided and poorly educated sheep. It wasn't all their fault they were clueless. That they were assholes was mostly on them, but the clueless part was on the school.

The only actual response I ever received to my argument that business could be anti-Jesus came from a business major I argued with on Facebook once. He said that Jesus never said anything about corporations or profit, so that meant he was pro-business. He did not reply to my mention that Jesus never said anything about homosexuality, so he must be pro-gay. Sad as this notion might be, it is the only attempt at an answer I ever encountered while at EVU. Of course, I've read books and articles on the matter. I always told my students that I wasn't anti-capitalism or anti-money. I often told them I hoped they would all someday be wealthy, and I meant it. That's the reality of the world we live in. It's sad that I can offer better explanations regarding money and wealth than graduating business students at EVU. But I would hope that with the possibility of great wealth there would be some introspection and philosophical musing about the nature of life. I found, over the fifteen years I was there, that asking students to consider the concept of wealth to any depth was asking too much.

Every semester in my Introduction to Literature class, I had students read a few stories that dealt with poverty and money. I wanted them to consider their views of money and wealth in relation to their faith. Given what Jesus said about money and greed, I asked them if it was okay for a Christian to buy a wildly expensive car, like a Bentley. Was it morally permissible for a follower of Jesus to spend $300,000 to $400,000 on a car? I never indicated either way what an acceptable answer would be. I just asked.

I would always have the students talk among themselves first. I didn't want to let their assumptions about me influence how much they shared of what they really thought. The students always took to the issue with enthusiasm. I would see small groups of three or four nodding and agreeing. Watching evangelicals rationalize questionable behavior that is foundational to their cultural understanding of their faith is fascinating. They clearly understood, if subconsciously, they were in murky waters. But as soon as someone offered any kind of argument in support of wealth and luxury, they agreed quickly and wholeheartedly, clinging to the thin thread of logic as if their life depended on it. Then we would have a class discussion to bring it all together.

"Jesus wants to bless us," one student might offer, eliciting a chorus of, "Yes!" and, "We just have to allow him to bless us." Most of the time, I resisted the urge to ask if the victims of tsunamis or wars simply did not allow God to bless them, saving that for another day.

Every semester I heard this thought expressed multiple times over: "As long as you can afford it and still be responsible, and as long as you also give the same amount of money to charity, then why not?"

Every year, some hapless student would use his or her own family as an example. "My dad runs a business and is always giving back to the community and to our church. He works hard for his money, so he deserves to drive any car he wants."

Sometimes the students even told the class what kind of car. "My dad bought a Ferrari last year, and it's awesome," one student exclaimed. I asked him if, when he bought the car, his dad cut a check for $300,000 to a charity or the church, since that was what he had argued. He didn't know. I always let it go sooner than I wanted to when students brought up their own families. I didn't want to go after them and their relatives in front of the whole class.

One of the most common and disturbing responses to this discussion was a student responding with utter contempt at me bringing it up. "If someone has the money to spend, then clearly God wanted him to have it," students have said throughout my time at EVU. This is the libertarian Christian view. It is part "prosperity gospel" and part "selfish asshole." And it's easily defeated. To this I always countered by asking if assassins and drug dealers were blessed with riches by God. Almost always, the student would rethink his or her statement and back down, hopefully going on to consider deeper views of life and faith. But every once in a while I encountered a truly honest, logical, and evil human being. When confronted with my query, the student would think for a second and then answer, "Yes." Part of the answer, I'm sure, comes from being called out on a fallacy in front of the entire class and the student not wanting to back down against me. The last time this happened, there were audible gasps from the students, even from the pro-Bentley crowd. But I actually wanted someone to express this idea, just so it would come into sharper relief. That really bad actors getting rich is okay was the only logical conclusion for anyone who subscribed to the "prosperity gospel."

In every class was a small group, usually BIPOC, who considered themselves progressive or liberal. They would sometimes jump into the prosperity argument and decry the expressions of greed and materialism, but mostly they just stayed silent and snapped their fingers when I called out the conservatives and libertarians. They would come up after class and thank me for bringing up the topic. Countless students have told me that I was the only professor they had at EVU to ever challenge the idea of wealth or greed. But in reality, I wasn't the only professor to do this. I know many colleagues who challenged power and examined assumptions of all types. But we were a fringe minority at EVU. All these experiences were enough to help me see how much evangelicalism is inextricably tied to capitalism and profit. It isn't just at EVU that this is assumed and promoted. But the gilded ivory tower, which pretends to promote academics and critical thinking, is a foundational component of evangelical culture that feeds into evangelical churches and communities.

## It Was Going to Happen Eventually

In my last couple of years at EVU, I got put back to being a one-year contract lecturer with only fifteen units of work, or five classes. My being downgraded from assistant professor, it was explained to me, was due to the understaffed English department finally hiring a couple of new people, which gave them more leverage to sideline me during this time when my involvement with the Multi-Ethnic Programs and the underground LGBTQIA group was going on, along with me just being me in the classroom. They knew all about my activities, thanks to students who complained and even students who were trying to support me.

In one of my last "visits" to the chairperson's office, I was handed a printout of an email sent to the school. In it, a mom detailed her daughter's experience where she ended up dropping out of EVU because she took a Shakespeare class, not with me, but with one of my colleagues. The mom expressed outrage that students were being allowed to read the filth contained in Shakespeare's plays, but this is not why she decided to write to the school. It turns out, the student had a good friend who was in my Freshman Writing Seminar and liked me. She tried to argue in favor of the school by saying she had learned so much from me and had even changed her faith to care about gay people. She still felt being gay was a sin, but she credited my class and the discussions we had as helping her be more caring as a Christian. This student modifying her approach to the queer community was the main complaint of the email.

Instead of helping, the student unwittingly gave the mom an even bigger issue to complain about: *me*. My colleague who taught the Shakespeare class was not named. I was. As "bad" as teaching Shakespeare was, encouraging love and compassion toward gay people was apparently the worst thing a professor could do.

My chairperson told me I had to be more careful because the department couldn't defend me. He then told me that at the end of the year, they were taking away my lecturer position, and I would be a lowly adjunct from that point on.

By this point, my friends and even some of my colleagues were asking me why I put up with such horrible treatment at EVU. One colleague even pulled me aside after a meeting and started crying, telling me she was heartbroken at everything the school had done to me.

I had risen from an entry-level adjunct to a one-year contract lecturer in three years. After a few years doing that, I was made a full-time assistant professor for the next five. I was demoted back to the lecturer position in the fall of 2010. And at that point my other options for teaching had dwindled. After five years of requesting classes to teach at a nearby college only to tell them I couldn't teach them when my full-time EVU contract was renewed, I had burned a bridge.

Up until 2012, I stayed at EVU because I still enjoyed teaching my classes. I loved creating space for discussions and seeing students experience that *aha* moment. I loved showing students who assumed they couldn't write that they could. I loved going through stories and texts and expanding worldviews. I had seen a few generations of students come to EVU as innocent evangelicals become galvanized as warriors for social justice, and I had seen them foment revolutions. Students I knew and loved had created artistic and activist spaces in an environment that hated them. From the Sisters Nine exploring language and identity under low lights and the faint smell of weed, to the LASA students unwilling to take the racism in the community or in the policies, to the APASO kids just learning to find their voices, to the GSA/Haven kids desperately trying to find their place, I had always found reasons to remain at EVU. While students often thanked me for supporting them, I felt a deep sense of honor and privilege to be there to witness their courage and their tenacity to fight for their place. From 2008 until those last couple of years, those students kept me going.

And by 2012, most of them were long gone, off into the world to pursue their own hopes and dreams. EVU clamped down on MEP after Joe Snell's death, installing a puppet director who would ensure school policies were enforced. There would be no more queer poetry, no more protests for cultural events, no more unrest among the disenfranchised. The LASA boys and the Cirelli sisters (Abbie had a sister, Liz, who had taken over Haven) had become so feared by staff and administration, new rules were put into place to censor the content of all events on campus. All content, songs, poems, speakers, and so forth had to be preapproved by Student Life staff. Violations would result in fines and termination of an organization.

I was in a planning meeting for what would be the last week dedicated to cultural and race awareness, UNLEARN Week, after Joe's passing, and there was a long discussion about what to do with LASA. The staff person acting as their faculty adviser assured the committee that she had LASA under control. No surprises that year, she promised. I told Matthew Gonzalez that I was both proud of him and LASA and pissed that the administration had made it impossible to put on events that could challenge anything at EVU. At first, the students got around the censorship by performing angry, anti-racist poems in Spanish, but the school countered by bringing in Spanish professors to snitch on them. I told the APASO kids to skip the preapproval process altogether, and that I would pay the $300 budget from the school they would lose by going on probation. But being the good, rule-following Asian Americans they were, they followed the rules.

At the end, APASO was so bled dry of life by all the new rules that even the students got sick of me always wanting to talk about their identities and race issues. After Sammie's generation, the Asian kids just wanted to hang out, play games, and get boba. All the talk of race and identity was too depressing. Not even my famous friends were impressing them anymore. In fall 2012, my last fall at EVU, we had a meeting talking about Jeremy Lin, the breakout NBA star who was the first Asian American to become famous in the NBA. I talked about how racism kept him out of the game for so long, even when he showed talent, and we talked about the perceptions of Asian American men. In the middle of what I thought was a great discussion, a kid raised his hand. He sighed heavily and asked why he needed to hear all this. He didn't think it mattered and we were just wasting time worrying about racism.

I was pissed. I told him he would one day be at a job interview, and he had better hope the person interviewing him didn't have racist views of Asian men. If Jeremy Lin couldn't convince people of his abilities even when he was scoring 38 points against the Lakers, how could this student expect to be assessed fairly? The kid just shook his head in the exact same way White boys shook their heads at me in my classes. I realized in that moment that APASO, the group that invited me to be their leader and that I had helped create, had given up on actually talking about being Asian.

At the last annual Asian Americans in the Media event, only twelve students showed up to hear Keiko Agena, Jenny Yang, traci kato-kiriyama, Patricia Ja Lee, and Kennedy Kabasares share their thoughts.

The Gay/Straight Alliance that became a group called Haven would rise in prominence right up until around this time. We had a brief falling out where the new leaders of the group disinvited me from coming to meetings because I expressed concerns about their plans to come out to the school. The kids wanted full acceptance from the school and the administration, and I told them they would never get it, nor should they aspire to getting acceptance from people who thought they were abominations. They, in turn, accused me of being too old and too cynical. It broke my heart. Those kids, in addition to figuring out their identities, also really wanted the school to love them fully. To them that was all-important, because EVU was their world. They didn't want to hear from me that the world was out there waiting for them with multiple communities to join and that EVU wouldn't mean shit to them when they left. They just wanted EVU's love and acceptance, even though it never happened.

After a couple of years of exile, I was welcomed back by the next generation of leaders. At its peak, Haven's Art Night would become one of the biggest events of the year at EVU, with hundreds of people attending. It even became "cool" to be associated with the group, with kids expressing their rebellious sides by wearing pride flags or pins and shaving their heads. I noticed a big change from my early days when the students' worst fear was to be perceived as gay. Now the cool kids were showing up to Haven events at what they called the House of Love, a house they rented off campus.

But even Haven felt like it had outgrown me. I had lost APASO, MEP was in its death throes, my department had stopped talking to me as I was no longer part of the "real" faculty, and I lost interest in connecting with students outside of my classes. It felt like the moment had passed, and I was alone in a place I no longer knew.

With my career in question, it was now just a matter of teaching as many classes as I could for income while I searched for employment elsewhere. I taught at a couple of other community colleges, but I just couldn't break in as a regular adjunct. Coming from an evangelical school where I taught for fifteen years was not a ringing endorsement for my abilities as an educator. But with the growing acceptance sinking in that I was on my way out, I grew bolder in my identity. When students filled out their evaluations of me at the end of the semester, and still as a teacher with good rapport with my students, I would tell them to write incriminating things like, "Professor Okamoto says he is right about LGBTQIA issues and the school is wrong." I told them to write ridiculous things about me, preferably with pictures drawn. If I was going out, I wanted Campus Security to come storming in to pull me out of a classroom, kicking and screaming.

What actually happened was, after the 2013 school year ended, I got a call from the dean's office. Done were the days of my chairperson calling me in. I was asked to come in the next morning to meet with the dean himself.

I spent the next twenty-four hours reminiscing. I thought of those first days of innocence as I clung to my faith. I thought of the Asian club, APASO, and how it had risen from a conservative, well-intentioned small group into a significant player in the rise of the Multi-Ethnic Programs and then steadily declined into a social group I had very little involvement with. I thought of the Sisters Nine and the inspiration they had given me. Ella Baker, when she graduated, had even gifted me with the water bong we had partaken of before many gatherings. I thought of Haven and the glimmer of hope in the eyes of the idealistic students who were also afraid of being discovered, and who were treated so cruelly by their families and community, driven to depression and suicidal thoughts. But I also thought of the Haven leaders like Abbie and Liz Cirelli, Glenda McDannell, and so many others who fought and actually changed school policies to at least protect LGBTQIA people from harm. I thought of the Latin American Student Association (LASA) boys who had successfully started a revolution and made actual changes to school policies. They forced the school to have Spanish translators at graduation and got the school to become an official Hispanic-Serving Institution. And I thought of all my students who had trusted me to not only teach them the English language but allowed me to broaden their perspectives on life and love in this cruel world.

And then I thought of my own family and community in absolute contrast to my world at EVU. Where life at EVU was a constant struggle to survive with any dignity and self-respect for myself, and a never-ending struggle to support the marginalized people all around me, my family and friends gave nothing but love and support to me and to everyone around them.

That night, about twenty friends showed up to an ice-skating rink to help a singer-songwriter friend shoot a music video. We skated around and around while the main story of the video played out, and I had a few hours to just revel in my community before going home to wonder what the dean would say to me the next morning.

When I arrived the next morning at the dean's office, my chairperson was waiting outside the door, looking visibly anxious. We went into the dean's office and exchanged pleasantries, but the dean got right to the point. He had a stack of folders on his desk, filled with complaints about me. He read a few of them out loud, and when he read, "Professor Okamoto says he is right about the LGBTQIA issue and the school is wrong," I cracked a smile. Of course that was one of the ones he'd find. My heart was pounding, not because I was nervous or afraid. Quite the contrary. I knew this was my moment.

"Do you find this funny?" the dean practically hissed.

"I do," I said evenly.

The dean paused for a second, suddenly unsure of the situation. I'm sure he expected me to be contrite or embarrassed, but I was sitting there smiling. I waited for him to finish, and he put down the folders and launched into a short speech about how I was a harm to the school. I stopped smiling.

I don't remember everything I said, but I remember feeling energized and inspired. I started with, "This school is on the wrong side of history," and I launched into my own speech about everything I had done for the school. On my own time I had supported APASO and all the MEP students. I had represented the school by presenting papers at national academic conferences like the Conference on Christianity and Literature and the Conference on Diversity in the Academy, which I helped start and organize with the Faculty of Color Group. In my classes I taught students to examine multiple views, and I pointed out that the complaints against me being prejudiced toward liberal views were just misguided. I had pushed everyone to analyze their views and biases, including the very few students who had identified as liberal. I asked him where all the student evaluations were that praised me for being fair, that thanked me for helping them clarify their views, or that helped them be better Christians. I had copies of hundreds of such evaluations, and I wondered why none of them were on his desk. For every one of those complaints there were dozens of compliments from the paying students of all backgrounds. Most importantly, I argued, my students knew I cared about them. Even the ones who didn't agree with me.

The dean was turning red, and I thought I saw his little brown mustache twitch. His voice was quieter, and he mumbled something about not being aware that I was actually teaching what I taught or that my relationship with students was so important to me. He had just read the negative things and believed them. Thinking back to the former campus pastor, this was definitely a pattern with White people in power. I chuckled to myself as I thought of all the actual things I had said and done that warranted firing. He seemed particularly upset that a student reported that I gave extra credit for using *fuck* in a sentence. All he had on his desk were opinions and a few examples that I, myself, had planted. It was fucking (adverb) hilarious. I had been hastening my own demise at EVU, and the dean had no idea.

The meeting was approaching the sixty-minute mark as we went back and forth, and the dean said he was late for another meeting. He sighed deeply and said he had come into his office to fire me, but to my surprise and to some satisfaction, he said that after considering everything I had said, he wanted me to remain as an adjunct. He also said he would like to observe my classes to make sure what I had said was the truth. He looked exhausted. Maybe I wanted to be fired, but I still wanted to fight.

My chairperson, who had been silent the whole time, walked me out of the building. He said something to the effect of me pulling off a miracle, and that he had never seen anyone change the dean's mind. I was just stunned because I had gone in ready to be fired, and here I was still employed with three Freshman Writing Seminar classes scheduled for the fall semester.

I told my wife, Geri, about the events of the day when she got home from work, and the first thing she said was, "Why on earth would you ever go back there?" She told me to just quit and stay home with our kids. It had been a logistical nightmare with three kids at three different schools, after-school activities, and my role as head cook. She was about to buy her family's dental practice and take over, and basically said my meager adjunct pay would be missed but not crucial to our family's survival.

So, I got up early the next morning and composed an email to the dean. It was seven pages of letting him and the school have it as I explained why I was leaving. Through tears, I recounted all the ways the school harmed non-White people, LGBTQIA people, women, and pretty much all of the faculty, who were underpaid and overworked.

All this measured against the accusation the dean had made to me that I was a "harm" to the school. In the end, I acknowledged that I was, indeed, a "harm" to the school. I was a "harm" to systemic racism and bigotry. I had come to the school in good faith in 1998, assuming that EVU was also against racism and bigotry only to find that it was not. In fact, it promoted it. So yeah. Harm to the school? That would be me, yes.

I then started composing an email to my department, thinking carefully about how to properly say goodbye. I wrote a much shorter note, thanking my colleagues for supporting me when I was new and reminiscing with the newer colleagues all the times we hung out in our homes and on the town. I apologized for all the negative attention I had brought upon the department, but I didn't apologize for who I was or what I stood for. It occurred to me that I was writing a letter no White professor ever had to write to the Department of English at EVU.

When I hit Send, I discovered in the ten minutes between sending the first email to the dean and sending this new message to my colleagues, I had been booted from the EVU system. I had heard from other colleagues that their accounts stayed active for weeks and months after they left EVU. The dean responded to my heartfelt resignation by immediately silencing me and ordering my erasure from all things EVU. I still wanted to send the note to my former colleagues, so I printed out copies and arranged via Facebook Messenger to have a colleague place them in the mailboxes of the English department.

Upon receiving the copies of my note by regular mail, my colleague chickened out and mailed them back to me with a note of his own, accusing me of making him my "errand boy" and telling me to just come to campus and distribute the letters myself. So great was the fear of being caught associating with me, my colleague wouldn't risk being caught placing my goodbye to my department into their mailboxes after fifteen years with them. I sure as hell wasn't going to set foot on campus, so the letter was never received by any of my colleagues.

In all, three of my English department colleagues reached out to me on Facebook after I quit, although more might have tried to reach out via my dead EVU email. I'll never know. Several people from other departments reached out with heartfelt expressions of sorrow and support. But the reality was, I was done at EVU after fifteen years, and aside from a few freshman students and a few colleagues, no one was going to miss me. I'm sure a lot of people, particularly in the School of Business and the "science" department, were thrilled I was gone. God had won.

The school had been both the setting and catalyst for my deconstruction of faith. It had also been both the impetus and the foil for my becoming a self-actualized Japanese American, progressive-minded man. Throughout the day of my resignation, I allowed myself to grieve the loss of some relationships and the legacy of the organizations I helped build, all of which were in decline and on their way to extinction. I thought of all the faces sitting in my classes, wide-eyed, sleeping, laughing, and frowning.

And then I thought of my community. After I announced my departure from EVU, I had let my non-EVU people know, and I received dozens of messages, celebrating, mourning, and just encouraging me. I may have finally left EVU, but I was embraced by my community who reached out to support me. I remember thinking everyone should have a day like this where all your friends tell you they love and respect you. I was prepared for leaving, but I was not prepared for this outpouring. I was losing a meager paycheck and stacks of papers to grade, but I was gaining my life. I had jumped out of all connection to anything Christian into the waiting arms of my community.

In the years that followed, I realized that just having worked at EVU still affected my identity. Despite being fully deconstructed from any religious faith, just being in that setting had colored my perception. The more time I spent outside of any evangelical space, the more I realized just how insidious and identity crushing that space was. Long before the 2016 election when evangelicals showed their hand and their hoods, I knew people like Donald Trump, who is no church boy, would always be loved and respected by evangelicals far more than BIPOC people like me who were raised in the church. Bigotry, ignorance, arrogance, misogyny, and hatred win big in those spaces.

All those years of fighting for my voice, my people, and for those around me gave me a chance to find my own identity. Clearly, I was the one who did not belong in that space. I was the one muddying the Whiteness, causing fundamentalists to feel uncomfortable, and advocating for good, ethical values completely at odds with evangelical Christianity. It was me that was "bad" or wrong. It was their house, and their rules I was breaking, even if they were inconsistent and generally unprincipled. My advocacy for the marginalized, my showing what the Bible says and doesn't say, and my very existence as a confident, passionate Japanese American man was subversive and criminal for fifteen years at EVU. And, goddamnit, what a ride.

⌘

Once I figured out how to define myself, I didn't care about catering to White expectations of who they wanted me to be. And once I deconstructed from religious faith, I was free to explore everything this life has to offer.

But I do not define myself simply by the things I have overcome. Being a Japanese American with a once-colonized mind, or one defined by Whiteness and power and success and money, will always be a reference point from which I strive to become a better person. And being a former evangelical Christian will always stand in stark contrast to the deeper and more expansive life I choose to live today. As a Christian, I feared so many basic components to a full life. While at EVU, my faith gave way to a life that embraced art and deep connections with so many different kinds of people of every kind of identity. The Christians, like my student who told me my marriage was somehow tainted by my wife's wild years as a teen, would have you believe the consequences to a life fully lived are guilt, shame, and death. Bullshit. They are lying to the world. A life fully lived based on mutual respect and love for everyone around you and for yourself is, well, you gotta try this. Embracing my identity, my sexuality, and my humanity has given me more joy, fulfillment, and sense of purpose than I ever had inside of Christianity.

Equally important to the past identities, which helped to shape who I am, is the mission to continue growing and building a new life apart from the past. I can be partly defined by life post-faith and post White-centered thinking, but I am, more importantly, defined by the life I choose to live and the people I choose to love and support.

In conclusion, my life fucking (adverb) rocks today.

# Epilogue

If there was ever a moment I thought about my past faith, it was two years after I left EVU. My wife, Geri, was diagnosed with breast cancer, and my world felt shattered. Once again, friends and family came through, caring for us and supporting us through the ordeal that saw Geri go through chemotherapy, surgery, and radiation over the better part of 2015. Through it all, I never once prayed. I expressed thanks for everyone caring for us, and I thanked people who told us they were praying for us, but I had passed my Jedi test. I was truly unsaved, dechristianized, disevangelicalized. And that part felt great.

EVU remained on my radar for a few years after I left, as you just can't turn off caring for something you spent so much time caring about. In the year after, EVU made national news by firing Donovan Ackley, a respected and beloved theology prof and chair of his department, because he returned from his sabbatical and announced he was a trans man. I went against my own judgment and regard for my mental health and returned to campus to help organize rallies on his behalf, and I even helped him clean out his office under the hateful eyes of everyone in the School of Theology.

I joined a Facebook group that supported the remaining LGBTQIA club that was trying to become a full-fledged student organization. The school actually allowed the group to be an official organization and removed its prohibition against same-sex relations in the student handbook. But naturally, local and national churches shit themselves upon learning of this, and mounted an attack on the school, so just weeks later it put the policy back. This resulted in organized attacks from groups like the Religious Exemption Accountability Project (REAP) and other LGBTQIA advocacy groups. It was all a familiar story, and though I wanted to be a help to the marginalized groups at EVU, I was moving on and forward more and more.

By this point, I was several years, Geri's cancer scare and full recovery, and two amazing bands removed from EVU. The more I focused on being a stay-at-home dad, playing music, and flourishing in my community, the less I found myself thinking about anything to do with evangelical culture. But it's a process—maybe something that will take generations to overcome.

I started writing stories from notes and journals with the hopes of writing this book, even before I left. A few friends from my old church and IVCF days had also left the faith, but I also began searching for connection with other apostates on social media.

I found the Exvangelical Facebook group in 2018, and there learned about a burgeoning community of ex-Christians and progressive Christians who no longer identified as evangelical. Through chats and various threads of discussion, I got to know Chrissy Stroop, Blake Chastain, and several others who had committed themselves to supporting ex-evangelicals. As the movement grew, and I found myself in virtual community with dozens of writers, activists, educators, and artists, all who had left evangelicalism for progressive Christianity, agnosticism, or atheism.

So, after seven years of peaceful living, completely untethered from anything to do with Christianity outside of my still-religious parents, I found myself right back in the fight to expose evangelicals as a global threat to peace and prosperity for all. Maybe I had the strength for it because I had indeed found a healthy distance and had found a new me. My experiences as a young evangelical and professor at EVU could be a useful resource for the movement. So I started a podcast about students and faculty at EVU called *Chapel Probation*, I've written this book, and I hope to do more.

I'm still close with my Tuesday Night Café community, even though the pandemic has canceled the past two seasons; and although Sugarcult broke up after its third album in 2008, I am still close with Tim.

Since starting the podcast, I have reconnected with many of the students I once worked with and fought beside. As we often say to each other, the experiences we shared fighting against the oppressive culture at EVU bonded us for life. Between them and the greater ex-evangelical community, my world continues to expand, teaching me, challenging me, and inspiring me.

May we all seek to build communities across borders, labels, and identities.

# Acknowledgments

I'm so grateful to have loving and supportive friends and family who inspire me to live fully and write honestly. They made deconstructing faith as smooth and lovely as it could have been, and they continue to make my life the most amazing adventure I could ever hope for.

Geri, my best friend and rock

Ethan, Audrey, and Owen, my kids who make me so proud

traci kato-kiriyama

Geneva Tien

Keiko Agena

Shin Kawasaki

Jenny Yang

Naomi Ko

Joyce Fujimaki

Daren Mooko

Atsuko Okatsuka

Sri Panchalam

Ryan Harper Gray

Tim Pagnotta

Jonathan Berry

My brother, Brian Okamoto

Craig Boyd

Joe Snell

David Morris

The Tuesday Night Café

The Deconstruction Podcast Peeps: Chrissy Stroop, Blake Chastain, Brad Onishi, Emily Torres, Cortland Coffey, Meghan Crozier, Zach Malm, the Dauntless Media gang (Nate Nakao, Gail Massarelli, Daniel White Hodge), Jo Luehmann, John Vernor, Tori Williams Douglass, Cindy Wang Brandt, Chad Shobert

The Mentors: Naomi Hirahara, Sarah Kuhn

The Bands: Band Moto (Dave, Jenny, Grace, and Paddy), B-Squad, Doctors and Engineers (Azeem, Jayson, Sri, and Sumi), Elephants with Guns (Jayson, Nik, Azeem, and Sumi), Bo Han Yang, Jen Lee

Whiskey Writing Wednesday crew

Neato Ito Writing Retreat crew (where this book began): Phil Yu and Joanna Lee, Jane Lui, Jenny Yang, Greg Watanabe, and traci

The SoCal Ex-Evangelicals: Brent Walmsley and Heather Owens

All the *Chapel Probation* guests

There are so many more friends who have been there for me during and after my time at EVU. So many conversations, observations, words of encouragement and support, and listening ears that have contributed to who I am. I am one fortunate fucker (noun).

# About the Author

R. Scott Okamoto is a fourth-generation Japanese American who lives in Pasadena, California, with his wife, Geri, and whichever kids haven't left the nest. He has an MA in creative writing from the University of San Francisco, and he taught university-level English for fifteen years. He enjoys fly fishing (and mostly fishes with the flies he ties), playing guitar, and cooking. He is the creator and voice of the *Chapel Probation* podcast. For more writing and videos of Scott speaking, and for photos related to the stories in this book, visit rscottokamoto.com.

www.ingramcontent.com/pod-product-compliance
Lightning Source LLC
Chambersburg PA
CBHW021717120626
46545CB00004B/1605